The Vietnam War:

An Untold Story of Drugs

Col William E. Campbell (Ret)

William E. Campbell, Colonel, USA Retired

The Vietnam War: An Untold Story of Drugs

ISBN-13: 978-1979146715
ISBN-10: 1979146713

Printed in the United States of America

First Edition

DEDICATION

This book is dedicated to those officers and soldiers
who served in the 90th Replacement Battalion
during the period covered here.

CONTENTS

ACRONYMS AND ABBREVIATIONS

AG	Adjutant's General
ARVN	Army of the Republic of Vietnam
CIF	Central Issue Facility
CWO	Chief Warrant Officer
DESPER	Deputy Chief of Staff Personnel
DESLOG	Deputy Chief of Staff Logistics
DEROS	Date Estimated Return Overseas
EM	Enlisted Man
FRAT	Free Radical Assay Technique
GI	Government Issue
KP	Kitchen Police
MP	Military Police
NCO	Non-Commissioned Officer
PX	Post Exchange
R & R	Rest & Recuperation
S-1	Staff Personnel
S-2	Staff Intelligence
S-3	Staff Operations
S-4	Staff Logistics
SAODAP	Special Action Office for Drug Abuse Prevention
TOC	Tactical Operations Center
UARPAC	United States Army Pacific
USARV	United States Army Vietnam
VC	Viet Cong

PREFACE

"One thing worries me. Will people believe me?
Will they want to hear about it?
Or, will they want to forget the whole thing ever happened?"

Lt. J.G. Richard W. Strandberg
US Navy Mekong Delta
May 16, 1968

The above quotation was taken from the Memorial to the Vietnam Veterans located in the Wall Street area of New York City. This memorial was dedicated on May 7th 1985, a full ten years after the last American departed Vietnam, and contains quotes from some 86 letters written during the conflict.

Richard was correct: People didn't believe, and worse yet, didn't care about Vietnam. Most wanted the war to be over so they could forget it. However, this conflict had a major impact on the American public—more than any of the United States' previous wars.

In recent times more and more is being written about the war in Southeast Asia. Some refer to it as America's twenty-five-year war. However, the United States government counted casualties only from 1961 through 1975. Most of the literature depicts Vietnam as a constant battlefield, never focusing on life in any other context. This story attempts to give the reader an insight into the drug scene in Vietnam during the later stages of the war. Many of the books now published refer to the topic. However, the emphasis of this account is what the government attempted to do to cure the men affected by drugs—a subject on which little, if anything, has been written.

According to Webster Dictionary, a "turnstile" is a mechanical device used to control passage from one public area to another. During the Vietnam War, the 90th Replacement Battalion was the "turnstile"—and the "public areas" were Vietnam and the United States.

My story begins when the replacement soldiers realize they are in Vietnam and will spend the next twelve months fighting the war. Their attitudes were combinations of apprehension and fear. The returnees, on the other hand, are happy, hateful, and, in some cases, "stoned" on drugs. The year 1971 is marked by an ever-increasing public outcry against this unpopular war, poor troop morale, high racial tension, and the phenomenon of Vietnamization—an ever-decreasing American presence in Vietnam, and ever-increasing evidence that more and more military people were hooked on drugs.

During the time frame of this account, President Nixon declares war on drug abuse in Vietnam. The 90th Replacement Battalion was given the mission of finding the users through urine analysis. At the same time, Vietnamization became a reality, and the strength of the American force drops from 250,000 to fewer than 70,000 troops.

The story covers the drug detection program and what it meant to the individual GI—how he reacted to being detoxified and delayed in leaving for home. It also focuses on the drug users and describes coverage by the press and the reactions— and visits— of congressmen. The story recounts how "clean" urine became a black-market commodity, and portrays how the people of the 90th responded to the drug user.

Along with the drug program came Vietnamization, making the 90th a very busy place. After six years of processing people, the battalion awoke one morning to an empty silence: a mission over. The story includes the sad effects of drug abuse, but it also recounts the comical moments that always seem to exist when men are thrown together with a shared goal of endurance and survival.

CHAPTER 1
ARRIVAL IN VIETNAM

M y 1971 return to Tan Son Nhut Airport, Saigon, was not as dramatic as my arrival there in June 1965. On the first occasion, about 168 of us deplaned from a Pan Am 707 into hot humid sunlight and entered the civilian terminal. Because so few Americans were in Vietnam at that time—only about 69,000—there was not yet a US military replacement area to process arriving soldiers. After deplaning, we 'newbies' were seated on wooden bleachers inside the civilian air terminal building, where a master sergeant began to deliver his canned introductory briefing on Vietnam. Ten minutes in, a loud explosion inside caused the bleachers to collapse, leaving us shocked. The sergeant was face-down on the floor, but amid the chaos, he picked up the microphone and said in a loud voice, "Welcome to the war zone, gentlemen!"

This book begins with my return to Vietnam on May 25th, 1971. Our 707 aircraft from Hawaii was preparing for landing at Tan Son Nhut. As the plane was making its approach to the Saigon area, I pored over the changes that had taken place in the nearly five years since I'd left. The airport was filled with fighter aircraft parked in concrete bunkers. The sky was full of helicopters; they looked like so many bees searching for pollen.

The bright silver of the C-130 cargo planes of 1965 was now

replaced with camouflage, and seemingly, hundreds of military people hurried around the terminal building.

My thoughts, however, were not on the scene below, but on the course of events that had brought me to Vietnam to be the Commander of the 90th Replacement Battalion. The 90th was one of two such groups stationed in Vietnam. It was headquartered at Bien Hoa, with one company, the 178th Replacement Company, stationed in Camp Alpha at Tan Son Nhut. The 22nd Replacement Battalion was headquartered at Cam Rahn Bay with a company at Da Nang. The mission was to process all replacements arriving in country to their assigned unit and to out-process all returnees to the United States. In addition, these battalions also processed people leaving the country on either R&R or leave.

I was coming to Vietnam from a two-year assignment in Hawaii. During my tour there, I had commanded the United States Army Pacific (USARPAC) Computer Center for approximately fifteen months and had been reassigned to the same headquarters as the personnel officer for the last nine. In the latter position, I was responsible for all personnel matters throughout the Pacific—with the exception of Vietnam. Upon returning to my office late in the afternoon on the eve of Thanksgiving 1970, I noticed on my desk the daily telex from Washington, DC with the names of the men within USARPAC who were being alerted of an upcoming tour in Vietnam. The first name on the list was mine! The reporting date to be in country was June 15, 1971. I thought Washington's personnel people were really getting good, positioning a lieutenant colonel for assignment eight months before his reporting date!

I went home that night but didn't tell my family because of the holiday. The following Monday, a call to the Adjutant's General assignment branch revealed that I hadn't been assigned anywhere yet, only that I was on deck. During the conversation, I learned that my best friend, Charlie Connell, had also been alerted to go at approximately the same time. We had served in Vietnam together in 1965 and 1966.

Charlie Connell and I had met in Washington while we were graduate students at American University. We were two of the eight captains slated to go to graduate school that year to learn data processing. Since graduation in 1963, we had both been confined to technical assignments in data processing. Being limited to one field of endeavor in the Army is tantamount to premature retirement. The Army's thinking is that for an officer to advance to the rank of colonel and above, that person must be well-rounded, working a varied number of jobs across many disciplines. At the time I got my alert orders, I was a personnel officer, but I had been in that position only a few short months after so many years of technical positions. I worried I would receive another tech assignment.

My first call to the Vietnam assignment officer in January was to ask what job he had in mind. He laughed at me, "Too early to tell you anything."

While I waited for news, I moved my family from Fort Shafter to a house off-post. My oldest child was to be a senior in high school that year, and my wife was graduating from the University of Hawaii in May. I didn't blame them for voting unanimously to remain in Hawaii during my yearlong deployment.

As February turned to March and then to April, I tried my luck once again with the assignment officer. I began by asking about the possibility of a divisional Adjutant General position. He let me talk for a while, then told me that I was scheduled to command the computer group responsible for strength accounting of US forces in Vietnam. My heart sank. Just the job I didn't want or need, not only because of its undoubted effect on my career, but because I had held the same job at Fifth Army in Chicago and in Hawaii.

The next couple of weeks were dark indeed. I racked my brain to come up with a way, any way, to get out of the data processing assignment. I even called the United States Army Vietnam (USARV) Adjutant General, Colonel Gardner. But he was adamant saying, "You're technically qualified, and the incumbent is due to rotate on June 15th It couldn't be a better match."

As late April arrived, a thought struck me—the 90th Replacement Battalion might be a possibility. I had worked with the unit at Fort Lewis, Washington in 1957. There the 90th had had the same assignment as in Vietnam.

In another call to the assignment officer in Vietnam, I expressed my desire to command the 90th Replacement Battalion. The officer was appalled; he thought I was crazy. He claimed the 90th Replacement Battalion was a graveyard for commanders. It had had eleven commanding officers (COs) in five years. Many had left without a favorable comment in their files. Anything and everything could go wrong in that type of battalion, and usually, it did. However, I'd made up my mind. Another technical job would end my career as a lieutenant colonel. The assignment officer promised nothing however, even though the present CO was due to rotate on June 15th.

I spent the next few weeks feeling sorry for myself. My

replacement in Hawaii had arrived, making me a lame duck. The only excitement in the Campbell household was that my wife had finished her final exams, making a perfect 4.0 during her two years at the University of Hawaii, and now she was about to graduate. Our seventeen-year-old son said, "Mom, if I studied as much as you do, the men in white would take me out with a coat that buttoned up the back!" My wife was now a trained dietitian.

Hoping for the best, I began running three miles a day and reduced my weight by ten pounds. I remembered the heat in Vietnam; being overweight would make it worse. And after jogging, I did sit-ups in the back yard.

One day, as I was bathed in sweat, my son arrived home with his school chums. One young lady asked, "Why are you working so hard?"

"I'm on orders to go to Vietnam," I answered.

"You're stupid to go!" she retorted. "You're a killer!" Then she left indignantly. I knew her father—a general officer at USARPAC Headquarters. Her response was one of the biggest shocks of my life. The rising public criticism of the war had penetrated the military's own households.

Forty years old, with eighteen years in the Army, I was becoming confused. I was going to a job I didn't want with no support from American civilians, including the sons and daughters of my fellow officers. The days dragged on. My replacement wanted me out as much as I wanted to begin my new assignment.

In early May I decided to plead my case with Colonel Gardner one more time. My call went right through to him without the normal blocking by his administrative assistant, which surprised me. I began my conversation along the usual lines, but before I could volunteer for the 90th again, he interrupted me.

"Can you be there by May 25th?"

I could.

"The 90th job is yours," he snapped. "Goodbye."

I doubted what I had heard. A call back to Vietnam uncovered the how and why of it all. The present battalion commander had been the first to serve a complete year, and he was scheduled for a sought-after assignment back in the States. If he didn't leave by May 30th, he wouldn't be able to take his thirty days' leave. There were no other Adjutant General lieutenant colonels due in the country prior to June 15th, so if I could come early, I had the command. So I threw the argument of my "technical proficiency" to the wind just to satisfy a departing man's desire for thirty days' leave. I really didn't care about the politics, only that I had the job.

The assignment officer confirmed it. "The computer job is going to be filled by Charlie Connell."

I went home to tell my wife.

"Good news, honey. I got the job."

"I'm happy for you," she answered, "but remember, May 25th is my graduation day." As luck would have it my plane departed late that night. The kids and I went to the graduation.

The bump of the landing gear on the runway brought me back to the reality that I was in Vietnam for my second tour of duty. As I got off the plane, I could see that Tan Son Nhut had been transformed. It was now a military base. MPs were everywhere, giving directions. Baggage was off-loaded in a hurry. I found out later that these civilian aircrafts would move back skyward quickly to avoid the possibility of Viet Cong mortar fire. On entering the same building as I had in 1965, I found further evidence that this was now a rather harried but efficient military operation. Uniforms were everywhere. Racks had been built for the baggage. MPs guided my every move, which they insisted must be done in a hurry. Most of the passengers would head for Camp Alpha where the people of the 178th Replacement Company would process them to their assigned units.

When I looked up, there stood Ed Clarke, the present CO of the 90th, the man I was to replace. He smiled broadly, and I could read his thoughts. "Sure glad you're here so I can go home." Along with Ed was another Lieutenant Colonel, Billy Cherry. The two men had been friends for years. Cherry and I had served together as Adjutant General advisors in Vietnam during 1965–66. Billy had attended American University one year ahead of me. He had volunteered to come back to Vietnam in the same advisory role he had had in 1966. Since Billy was a techie, fighting the same confining assignments, he too was trying to broaden his experience. Ed Clarke, on the other hand, couldn't spell *computer*, and didn't want to learn. Ed was considered a "comer" in the Corps and a sure bet to go on to general officer.

The greetings were warm. Because I was wearing a khaki uniform and they were dressed in combat fatigues, it was obvious who was new to Vietnam; I endured the good-natured ribbing all newcomers receive. Ed picked up my bag and headed to the parking lot. We all three got into Ed's jeep—Ed at the wheel, and Billy took shotgun. The back seat, with its utter lack of suspension, was all mine.

As we drove through the front gate of Tan Son Nhut, Plantation Road evidenced some surprising changes. I had traveled this way each day during 1965–66 to get from Cholon, where I was billeted, to the Vietnamese High Command, where the Adjutant General and the other Vietnamese Army staff were headquartered. Plantation Road is a two lane road with huge poplar trees on either side. It offered a picturesque view but could not be practically expanded, nor was it safe if you got run off the road, which would happen now and then. In 1965, the land along both sides of the road was mostly undeveloped: except for a French cemetery for war dead, it was a stretch of open field. Boys would fish in the ponds that developed during the rainy season. I never understood what they could possibly catch.

By 1971, both sides of the road had been built up with shanties about five feet high and constructed from tin sheets bearing the names of every brand of American beer. As the fighting had increased in intensity in the countryside, Saigon's population had swelled. Mama-sans squatted outside the shanty openings. Children darted between the stalled traffic, many of them not yet toilet-trained and naked from the waist down. The bars and bar-girls along the road were too numerous to count. The cemetery might have been out there somewhere, but it was impossible to see anymore.

We crawled a few feet and stopped. Where once donkey carts and bicycles filled the roadway, new trucks and thousands of Honda motor scooters choked traffic. The Japanese had modernized the Vietnamese mode of transportation, and the result was gridlock. Motor scooters going east and west worked their way one by one around the ones going north and south. Somehow, they managed to move along in a slow way and with a minimum of shouting and horn blowing. I often wondered what would happen under similar conditions in my hometown of New York City.

We finally made our way out to Route 1 and turned north toward Bien Hoa. The scenery was not much changed along the roadside except the small roadside stands that had sold vegetables and fruits in 1965 now offered tires, gas, and oil. But the makeup of the traffic and the speed at which it travelled were new to me. Route 1 was a four-lane concrete highway, probably the only one in Vietnam. Once in traffic, Ed increased his speed to fifty miles per hour, and it was as if we were standing still. Traffic passed in a steady stream. Motorcycles had only one speed—as fast as they would go—and continually cut in and out of slower-moving traffic. The Vietnamese military now drove newly provided American military vehicles. Every two-and-a-half-ton truck that passed us was missing one tire from each dual set on the back and looked as if it might have seen duty with General Patton twenty years earlier. There was a yellow line down the middle of Route 1. This, however, meant nothing to the Vietnamese. If there were two vehicles side by side heading in the same direction and another wished to pass, it was routine for the passing vehicle to cross the yellow line into the oncoming traffic and overtake the other two.

Both mesmerized by the sight and terrified that I might never reach my new assignment, I pondered the situation. In 1965, to keep American strength down and to help the Vietnamese economy, the government had imported trucks without GI drivers. The plan was to hire drivers from among the locals, but no one had thought to ask if the Vietnamese *could* drive! After realizing their error, the Americans built a driving school off of Plantation Road. So here we were, five short years later, and it seemed as if every person had his own motorized vehicle. I began to think that the course had neglected to cover the chapter devoted to the rules of the road.

Ed guided the jeep up Route 1, and we finally arrived at the entrance to the 90th Replacement Battalion—right off Route 1 opposite the village of Bien Hoa. Since the 90th had arrived toward the end of my first tour and was then located at Camp Alpha, I had never been able to really picture it at Bien Hoa. When we reached the front gate, however, I recognized the area. During the early part of my previous tour, it had been jungle and banana plants. Later, an artillery outfit from the 1st Division moved in and began to construct the buildings which now housed the 90th.

Our jeep's arrival prompted snappy salutes from the two MPs and other people standing around the gate. Ed called out the names of most and was greeted with friendly comments. He was a tough but fair commander and it was obvious he was well-liked. I wondered how I would be viewed. All eyes, of course, were on me. From the back seat, I could feel the stares and could guess what was running through their minds.

Front Gate – 90th Replacement Battalion

Ed drove forward. I saw that there were buildings off to the left that looked like barracks. To the right was an officers' club. The macadam road dropped off gently across a culvert through which a trickle of water was running, and then came up to a fork in the road. At the fork stood a decommissioned 105 Howitzer, a landmark left over from the artillery unit that had been based on the compound prior to the 90th's arrival. Taking the right-hand fork, Ed looped around some buildings and drove up to a high-fenced area.

He stopped the jeep. "This is home."

The sun was now very high in the sky, and perspiration started to trickle down my back. As we got out of the jeep, the GI guard at the gate gave a big smile and saluted. As for the smile, Ed explained that to protect the outer perimeter he was authorized to hold back eighty infantrymen for up to fifteen days; this guard would thus spend fifteen fewer days in the bush, and he was showing his appreciation.

The battalion staff officers' compound was made up of five trailers—the civilian kind you'd see in the States. Three were arranged in a U pattern around concrete pad, and at one end of the pad was a brick barbecue pit covered by a plastic roof. Two other trailers stood on the other side of the commander's trailer.

Inside the compound, the Executive Officer and the Operations Officer lived in one trailer and the Commanding Officer in another. The third had been condemned, but there was no way to move it out, since the eight-foot-high wooden fence held it prisoner. In the fourth trailer lived the adjutant and the supply officer. The fifth housed the special services women assigned to the battalion.

Ed's was a two-bedroom model. The front bedroom was to be mine until Ed's departure. In the closet were five sets of new jungle fatigues and two sets of jungle boots. While Ed and Billy talked, I changed into my fatigues and boots. I wanted to get out of the khakis to blend in better. I was determined to lose the newbie image, but it wasn't simple. New jungle fatigues and boots set me apart when I stood next to Ed, whose fatigues had faded with use and whose boots had darkened with wear. I was still the new guy.

After lunch in the mess hall, Billy said goodbye and headed for Saigon. Ed and I headed to the battalion headquarters building to meet the staff.

To my surprise, I discovered that Major Weeks, the executive officer, was due to rotate only days after Ed's departure. His replacement, Fred Meyers, had already arrived, and the two officers were busy reviewing a mound of paperwork. Fred was a soft-spoken black officer whose hometown was Foxborough, Massachusetts. He was in excellent shape. As I was later to discover, Fred jogged every day—whatever the temperature. He never drank anything stronger than grapefruit juice. There was always a case of the stuff in the refrigerator.

The operations officer had already departed. His replacement would not arrive until August. It seemed strange to have such a key spot vacant for such a long time. Ed assured me that the acting S-3, Captain John Holt, was a good man. He had moved to the S-3 position from being a battalion company commander. John was another mild-mannered officer with a dry sense of humor.

The adjutant, Phil Enright, was short, stocky, bald, and a Texas A&M graduate. He was never at a loss for words and always seemed to say the right thing to get people to laugh. His trailer mate, the supply officer, was a young captain named George Wills. George always looked as if he'd had a tough night, but was a typical supply type—he had all the right connections to get what we needed.

I spent the afternoon talking with the staff officers, discussing their tasks and operations, and meeting the enlisted people who worked with them. The group was impressive. But after a few hours, the fatigue of the trip began to drag on me—those who have made the trip to Vietnam know just how out-of-sync your internal clock can get. I excused myself and headed for the trailer. Before falling asleep, I prayed for the strength to command the battalion.

CHAPTER 2
LEARNING THE ROPES

Ed was due to depart for the States on May 29th, so he had only two days to show me the ropes. I awoke the morning after my arrival at 0230, the same hour I would awake for the following week until my body clock got on Vietnam time. Of course, it was too early to rise, so I dozed fitfully until it was time to get started. Three hours later I got up, dressed, and went to the mess hall of the 259th, the outfit responsible for out-processing enlisted men returning to the United States.

It was a huge building with one large kitchen and two separate dining halls: one large hall for the transients and a small dining area for the personnel of the 259th. The mess sergeant toured me through the kitchen where the cooks were beginning breakfast. The kitchen was orderly and clean, and all the kitchen police (KPs) were Vietnamese. The smell of eggs and ham made my stomach growl. By the time I had been seated at one of the four-man tables, Ed joined me. We had breakfast and discussed what was to fill the day. Our plan was to head to USARV Headquarters to meet my new boss and the assignment officers, because the battalion worked closely with them. Ed also wanted me to meet the Adjutant General, Colonel Gardner, and possibly the Assistant Chief of Staff for Personnel, Brigadier General Martin. Since Gardner and Martin were both Adjutant General Corps officers, I had met them before.

In his desire to impress me, the mess sergeant had filled my tray with too much food, and I felt bad about the heap of leftovers on my plate. As Ed and I walked out to his jeep, I realized he had an enlisted driver. I thought this extravagant. I would rather drive myself, anyway—especially when I had to venture down Route 1. I wanted to control my own destiny.

The trip to the Headquarters was about five miles, all inside the wire that surrounded the USARV area called Long Binh. The 90th Replacement Battalion itself was situated between the outside protective wire and the ammunition depot. Long Binh's size was overwhelming. The area didn't exist—at least not on the same scale—when I left Vietnam in 1966.

On the way, we passed different points of interest which Ed pointed out. The finance center was a huge edifice the size of a college field house. We passed a great number of two-story wooden barracks which housed the enlisted men of the different staff elements and units stationed at Long Binh. Next came a sea of trailers just like the one I had slept in. Ed noted that these were for field-grade officers—majors, lieutenant colonels and colonels. It looked as if there were enough to house all the field-grade officers in the entire army. Then we passed the building where the computer installation was housed. It was hard to distinguish this as a building since there was a wall of sandbags all around it. It was to be Charlie Connell's place of business in about three weeks. Charlie later grew to hate that sandbag wall—because of Vietnam's weather, the covering tended to rot quickly, creating a need for constant repair. At the time I didn't know that the 90th would need sandbags in other places as well, and I'd later learn to hate the sandbags too.

We passed the general officers' mess, which strongly resembled a New England hunting lodge. Surrounding it were cottages built to match, designated for the commanders, senior officers, generals and colonels holding staff jobs at USARV. Past the generals' mess was what people called Pentagon East, the USARV Headquarters building. Three stories high, it looked as big as the Pentagon. When we got closer and I saw the macadam parking lot and cement sidewalks, I was impressed with its construction—better than many of the army posts that I had served on in the States. Moreover, the Headquarters building had been designed without a single light switch. At night it was lit up like an office building from the pre-energy crisis New York skyline. Unbelievably, in the years it was occupied by Americans, not a single V.C. mortar round found the mark.

The driver let us off at one of the side doors, and we walked up to the third floor. On the way down the corridor, I ran into officers and sergeants I had served with over the years. Each was in a hurry, having just time enough to say, "I'm in room so and so. Stop by!" before they dashed off. Ed and I headed for a small office in the middle of the building.

There I was introduced to Colonel West, Ed's boss and the head of all enlisted and officer assignments in Vietnam. Colonel West was due to return to the United States a few days after Ed. His replacement, Colonel Lewis, sat at the desk across from West. Colonel Lewis would be my boss for the coming year. He had been last stationed in Hawaii, but he hadn't worked at USARPAC and I'd only met him socially.

For my benefit, a fellow lieutenant colonel briefed me on how the assignment branch affected the battalion. When soldiers arrived, my people would have them fill out various forms and would collect their personnel records. No one was supposed to leave the battalion to contact the assignment personnel directly. (This rule, though, turned out to be broken many times as assignment people came to get a friend out for the night.) Some assignment personnel lived and worked in the battalion area, and they were responsible for presorting records and calling information to USARV. The idea was to move soldiers to their assigned units within two days. The battalion handled all enlisted men and officers up to and including the rank of lieutenant colonel; colonels and higher weren't processed through the battalion.

People leaving country got their reassignment orders at their unit in Vietnam, and I was responsible for booking them back to the States. Ninety-five percent would be returning to Travis Air Force Base outside San Francisco, but those getting out of the service would be processed out at Oakland. About five percent, however, would return to McGuire Air Force Base outside Fort Dix, New Jersey. There would be two or three planes per month going to McGuire. It all seemed organized—but I didn't realize then what a pain in the ass those East Coast flights would become.

Smoking cigarette after cigarette, Colonel Lewis sat through the briefing and seemed to be a nice chap. I considered myself a heavy smoker, but Lewis was in another league. After the briefing, Colonel Brean led me on a tour through the third floor, where the assignment division was set up. The first office we entered was the biggest I had ever seen. Desks were arranged side by side, four or five on one side of the aisle and the same number on the other. They stretched for a good thirty rows. Over three hundred people worked in the room. It turned out there were three such offices.

The workload was divided up by rank of specialist-four, another composed of non-commissioned officers, another of company-grade officers, another of field-grade officers, and a smaller group of colonels. The sight of all those poor bastards at their desks made me thankful for my job.

I saw a lot of familiar faces. It took me two hours to walk the gauntlet, chatting with officers and NCOs. Some I hadn't seen in years, and I spent a good twenty minutes going over old times with one, Jack Dickey. Jack had been at MACV Headquarters during my tour in 1965–66. As an Adjutant General Corps officer, he was responsible for MACV postal matters. Jack had majored in postal for about ten years but was now in charge of NCO assignments. I served with Jack again after I got back to the United States. Jack was charged with developing a new personnel system for the Department of the Army, and I managed the programming staff that produced it. When the system was finally ready, Jack and I would travel all over the world to brief the personnel. We did a 'Huntley-Brinkley' routine, and Jack would introduce me as the Innkeeper of Holiday Inn East. This would always get a loud, friendly round of boos.

By now it was lunchtime. We all went to the officers' club— Clarke, West, Lewis, Brean and me. The club was large, and the chow was extraordinarily good compared to the fare in 1965, a steady diet of fried chicken and hamburgers. Our talk was mostly about home. Three times Lewis grubbed a cigarette from me. He professed to be a little embarrassed, but desperate. This was the beginning of months of supplying Lewis with cigarettes. His officers ran a pool each day to see how many butts would be in the ashtray by 10 o'clock. I got in on the pool a few times myself.

The young captain who worked in the office outside Lewis' would go in at 10 and carefully clean out the ashtray while others would distract his boss.

After lunch, I met with Colonel Gardner and his deputy, Colonel Davidson. Both later became major generals. The talk in the afternoon centered on the necessity to fill every seat on all aircraft returning stateside. The Deputy Chief of Staff, Logistics, was responsible not only for ordering the correct number of planes for the month, but also for anticipating the peaks and valleys. Empty seats were not to be tolerated.

The reports DCSLOG relied upon came from the Adjutant General, and the automated strength reporting system had not been reliable since late 1965. I was not connected with the process then, but Charlie Connell had been. The buildup ordered by President Johnson had come on so rapidly that the automated system had been overwhelmed. In 1965, strength accounting was processed on two UNIVAC 1005s, very early and rather limited computers. The idea was to process an update cycle every night, adding and deleting people. By late 1965 and early 1966, the processors were so overburdened that the unit was lucky to process four cycles every month. In my job commanding the personnel accounting computer unit in Hawaii, I had been responsible for a backup site that stored Vietnam's monthly report tapes. The computer processor at both sites was now a Burroughs 3500.

In an effort to help out the unit in Vietnam, we used to print out their tapes and review them for obviously invalid records — such as people whose date due to return from overseas, DEROS, was six months to a year past. There were always many of these. And because of uncertainty of the automated data, the USARV Adjutant General had manual reports coming from all field units indicating how many people were to rotate each day per month.

Using the automated and manual reports, and a little Kentucky windage, four majors from DCSLOG and the Adjutant General's office would order the planes. Amazingly, they were usually right. They should have gotten awards, but mostly they were fighting for their careers because of one or two bad days. It was also impressed upon me that if I didn't have enough people to book on planes coming in the following day, I was to contact local units— like the 1st Cavalry Division—and get as many people with upcoming rotation dates to the battalion right away. Colonel Gardner pointed out that General McDowell, the USARV Commander, gave the DCSPER and DCSLOG grief if planes went out with vacancies. It was one of the 90th Replacement Battalion reports he would review each morning at his staff meeting, and almost nothing got his Irish up as much as an empty seat.

Colonel Gardner tried to get time with General Martin, but his calendar was full. Ed and I got back to the battalion at about 1700 hours. The officers were having a combination farewell/hello barbecue that night for the two of us. It was to be cooked on the grill in the staff's compound. The battalion had a food service warrant officer overseeing all four mess halls—the three at Long Binh and one at Camp Alpha. Oddly enough, his name was the same as mine — Bill Campbell. Well, CWO Campbell had been around the army a few years, and I don't believe there was a mess sergeant in all Vietnam who hadn't been taught by or worked for CWO Campbell at some time during his career. I was expecting franks and hamburgers. But, that night's meal was as good as the best restaurant stateside. Campbell produced steaks, salads, cheeses, ribs, corn on the cob, and someone came up with a case of French wine.

Over the course of the evening, I met some of the officers assigned to the battalion, including the commanding officer of the 178th Replacement Company at Camp Alpha, Major Bill Huff, a soft-spoken man with a good sense of humor. Most of the officers assigned to the 90th were from the Adjutant General Corps, with the exception of the security platoon leader. His branch was Infantry, and he had seen combat in Vietnam. Most of the officers were ROTC graduates serving their obligatory two-year tours. There were only two majors—Fred Meyers, the executive officer, and Bill Huff, the CO of the 178th Company. All the others were captains and lieutenants. To my surprise, there was not a single familiar face in the group.

The evening ended early, and Ed and I made our tour of the battalion to ensure everything was quiet. Returning about midnight, I was more than ready for bed. My internal clock, I felt, was now on Guam time; in a couple of more days I should be okay.

The next morning Ed and I ate breakfast at the 18th Replacement Company mess hall, which fed the newly arrived enlisted men. The building was new and made of metal, and there was not a shred of insulation in the roof. It was a hothouse. CWO Campbell had his cooks working efficiently and the place was clean as a whistle, but it was so warm that it was not a pleasant place to eat.

At breakfast, Ed told me the story of the building—an anomaly amid the usual wooden structures. About nine months before, the wooden mess hall had burned to the ground. The fire started somewhere in the kitchen and the entire building was ablaze in a short time. A call was put into the Long Binh fire department. The fire trucks, manned by Vietnamese, arrived quickly. After running out the hose, they turned on the water. What followed could have been a sequence from a Buster Keaton film. The pressure was so great and the fireman handling the nozzle was so light that when the water began to flow, the hose began to toss him around like a basketball. Everyone and everything but the burning mess hall got wet. Ed said that he and other members of the 90th had finally stepped in, but by that time, the mess hall was a goner. The worry was the potential danger to the surrounding barracks. Ed said the heat was so intense that if one of the barracks started to burn he would lose that entire side of the compound. So they turned the hoses on the barracks, and the only building lost was the mess hall. It was a strain, feeding all the enlisted people in one mess, and quick action by the engineers got him the new metal mess fairly quickly. I was willing to bet, however, that none of those engineers would have cared to eat there.

Even apart from the discomfort, the headcount passing through this mess hall had fallen off appreciably during the last nine months. The high-water mark of troop strength in Vietnam had been 544,000. Now it stood at approximately 270,000 and was still falling. At this point I didn't realize how fast the strength would diminish during my tour of duty.

After breakfast, Ed and I retired to his office, where he briefed me on the battalion's make-up. There were five companies. The Headquarters Company was housed just inside the front gates. The staff to the battalion were assigned to this company. The 18th

Replacement Company was responsible for processing newly arriving enlisted people. The 259th Replacement Company was charged with out-processing all returning enlisted people. The 381st Replacement Company was the officers' processing company, and its role differed from that of the other two companies in that its mission was to process both in and out. Located at Camp Alpha in Saigon, the 178th Replacement Company was responsible mainly for processing people going on leave, and rest and recuperation—R&R in Japan, Australia, Hawaii, Taipei, and Bangkok.

When Ed figured I had all this down, he showed me the briefing charts hanging on the opposite wall. These charts supported the "canned briefing" used to give visitors the overall picture of the battalion. The talk began with the organization and staffing of the battalion. Its strength was approximately 350 GIs, but what surprised me was the number of Vietnamese the battalion employed. There were nearly as many Vietnamese employed as there were GIs assigned. The next portion of the briefing involved statistics, such as how many people processed in or out each month and how many people took R&R and where they went. The last part described the services we offered the transients, such as the clubs and the PX. I was surprised at the amount of money the PX took in. A typical month saw a profit of about $300,000.

As Ed finished the briefing, I was impressed with how clear it made things, and I resolved to spend some time looking over the charts to become as proficient as he was.

Just then, I noticed a convoy of buses pulling into the battalion area. Ed said it was a planeload of new arrivals who had just landed at Bien Hoa Airport. They had come from Travis Air Force

Base in California. He suggested we follow them through their processing. As the troopers got off the bus, they were ushered into a large building. They were seated two to a table, and their personnel records and orders were then collected. They filled out forms for their ration cards. Certain items, such as cigarettes and liquor, were rationed in country. The reason was to stop black-marketing. Those who were missing identification cards or dog tags also filled out special forms so we could give them new ones before they left. There were the usual warnings about the various intractable strains of VD and some warnings about punishments for dealing in the black market.

The men were then taken to the mess hall. The funny thing about the mess halls in the 90th was the lack of fixed hours, especially in the 18th Replacement Company mess. Sometimes an unannounced plane would arrive, and CWO Campbell would have food ready. One day when I asked him why we never seemed to have ham, he took me to the kitchen and opened the refrigerator. Inside there were twenty canned hams. This was how he survived two hundred or so unannounced guests dropping in for lunch—by hoarding canned ham. Every time he was sent ham, rather than serve it, he would substitute something else for it.

From the mess hall, the new arrivals were taken to the 18th Supply Room, issued bedding, and assigned bunks. That's where Ed said, "That's how they're handled when they arrive. Now, let's take a look at a group getting ready to go to their units."

We walked across the main battalion street to a large open field. He introduced me to Sergeant Moore, who was about ready to conduct a formation. Sergeant Moore was in his second tour with the battalion. He had spent his first one with the 90th during

1968–69 and had volunteered to come back.

Sergeant Moore mounted the podium. The new arrivals stood in formation in front of him. Like me, the troopers all looked new and somewhat out of place, dressed in new jungle fatigues and boots. As he called out a man's name, Sergeant Moore would wait for an answer and then call out the unit the man was going to. Sometimes there would be a cheer, but mostly there were groans. Each man would leave the formation, get his gear, and reassemble under the wooden shed behind the podium.

Soldiers going to local units waited in the shed to pick the men up. In about thirty minutes, a panoply of army vehicles began to appear. Troopers going up or down country by air would check the schedule board for the buses to Bien Hoa and the airport. People whose names weren't called out were put on details in the battalion or were marched off to complete their processing. At this time, the processing even included a fluoride treatment. Each man was issued a toothbrush with a fluoride container and would be watched while he applied the bad-tasting stuff.

We left the shed and walked through the 18th Replacement Company's barracks—the usual two-story army structures. Between each was a mortar shelter, consisting of construction pipe surrounded by ancient-looking sandbags. Ed said, "These little gems will have your ass in constant hot water with the Inspector General." He launched into a tirade against the makers of sandbags. He figured the company making them was screwing the military by overcharging and producing the cheapest possible materials. Almost every one had deteriorated and most of the sand was now on the ground. I asked when these had last been replaced.

Ed looked at me with scorn. "About four months ago. Those newbies you saw go off on detail this morning are probably filling sandbags. It's a never-ending battle."

We jumped in Ed's jeep and rode up to the 381st, located inside the front gate. The processing building was small but set up with two-man tables—like the 18th Company. There was one two-story billet that housed some of the 90th officers, as well as a number of single-story buildings that could sleep twenty-five to thirty people. Captain White, the CO, had just begun to address some officers due to depart on the evening plane. Ed and I sat in the back so I could listen. After it was over, Captain White gave me a tour.

Then Ed and I went next door with Captain White to have lunch in his mess hall, which was in the back of the same building that housed the officers' club. Captain White would be rotating in a few months. The mess hall was a pleasant place—another tribute to CWO Campbell.

After lunch, Joe Stanley, the commander of Headquarters Company, joined Ed and me for a tour through his area. Joe was a very serious-minded guy who wanted everything perfect—not a bad talent to have in a company commander. He had the troops' quarters in good shape. Behind his orderly room, he had a volleyball court, horseshoe pits, and four goats. I asked about the goats. "They keep the grass cut." I caught Ed with a half-smile on his face. He shrugged his shoulders.

The next morning, Ed took me to the orderly room of the 259th Replacement Company, commanded by Captain Nelson. Vic Nelson was a short, very stocky guy who had been in country about nine months. It occurred to me that in about two months, almost every officer and NCO will have turned over.

Nelson showed me around. His buildings were all low-slung single stories, each surrounded with fifty-five-gallon drums packed with sand and topped with concrete. This was to prevent mortar fragments from piercing the buildings. Ed pointed out that the barracks were built close together; if we ever had a fire, we would probably lose the entire company.

Returnees would arrive at the front gate either singly or in truckloads. Usually the single returnees were dropped off by a buddy, but one ingenious trooper rappelled from a helicopter and disappeared into the crowd before he could be caught. Less daring troopers came through the MP point at the gate. Officers would be directed to the 381st. Because of the uneven flow, the enlisted people queued up in bleacher-type seats under a big shed. Periodically, a processing NCO would brief the group and give them forms to fill out. These forms were important—people were booked on aircraft based on their DEROS and according to the time they entered the battalion. If for some reason you ever mistakenly booked someone out of turn, there was trouble. It seemed every person who passed through the 90th Replacement Battalion knew exactly what time every other soldier had arrived.

After the processing NCO finished his brief, he directed the people to the orderly room for bunk assignments. Ed suggested we follow along to see how this worked. We entered the processing shed next to the bleachers and to my surprise, I noticed a key punch machine. I asked Ed about it.

He replied, "How the hell do you think we can enter the data into the computer?"

"What computer?"

"The one next door."

We went into the Quonset hut next door. There was a UNIVAC 1005 card processor. I was shocked to see only a single window air conditioner that had to serve the entire building. There was a lot of dust and dirt around. Ed introduced me to Sergeant Whitehead, an experienced data processing man. I asked how he could possibly keep the computer running. He said he really didn't know, but that he hadn't called a maintenance man in months. He went on to say that the battalion wasn't authorized to have data processing people. He had trained two young troopers to operate and program the machine—one of them was a minor league baseball player in the Chicago Cubs' farm system, and he was learning a trade for his days after baseball.

As Ed and I walked through the different areas, I kept stepping on small plastic vials about 2 inches long. At first I didn't say anything, but eventually curiosity won out and I asked Ed. Ed, without batting an eye, said, "That's what heroin comes in." We started to discuss the drug problem. Ed said that many of the troopers that came through on their way home were hooked on drugs. Some would be glassy eyed; others would have lost a tremendous amount of weight.

"Where did they get the drugs, and how did they get them into the battalion?" I asked.

He said that the vials probably came in through the front gate, notwithstanding the shakedown. The GIs could be tremendously sneaky.

"I think a lot of it is sold inside the compound by the Vietnamese who work here," he added.

"How much does a vial go for?" I asked. The heroin in the vials, at that time, was 98 percent pure, and Ed believed the going price was $2 to $3 a vial. He figured the street price of the same amount of heroin back in the United States was $50 or $60, or more.

As we continued our tour, I began to watch people more closely. As Ed pointed out, many seemed disheveled and disoriented. In some cases, they were pugnacious. These may have been the ones trying to quit cold-turkey.

The day melted away. Ed and I made another tour that evening and then went to bed early—around 11 o'clock. He said that he ordinarily didn't get to bed until early morning, only after making sure everyone was asleep. This was a difficult task, as the battalion didn't ever seem to sleep; the new arrivals worried about what was facing them and those going home were so keyed up that they stayed awake, too.

The next afternoon Ed, the battalion staff officers, company commanders, and I practiced the change-of-command ceremonies that were to be conducted the following morning. We rehearsed on the field ordinarily used for the incoming enlisted personnel. The entire battalion was supposed to show up, all except for the company down in Saigon, which was going to bring up one platoon. That evening Ed went over to USARV Headquarters to have dinner in the general officers' mess, with General McDowell and the staff. This was the usual way for local commanders to leave Long Binh and Vietnam—by having their last meal at the general officers' mess.

The next morning dawned cloudy, and spitting rain. We had to decide whether to have the ceremony out on the field or indoors. If we did it inside, we would have to use the Central Issue Facility, where all the clothing and equipment issued to the new arrivals was stored. Ed and I decided we had better call off the outside ceremony and bring it in, because people had to move big crates and boxes around to make room for a very constricted battalion formation. Naturally, once we'd made that decision, the sun decided to come out for the rest of the ceremony.

Change of command ceremonies embrace pomp and circumstance. Standing between Ed and me, General Martin did the honors. The highlight was the passing of the battalion colors, which the sergeant major handed to Ed. Ed then passed them to General Martin, who then passed them to me. I now was the commander of the 90th Replacement Battalion.

After the formalities, Ed took the rest of the day off, hoping to get out on the plane leaving late that night. However, when we manifested the plane, Ed had just missed it. There were two hundred seats, and Ed was number 202. It would have been easy for me to bump somebody off and make sure Ed caught his flight, but I decided that if I was going to play by the rules, I might as well start right now. I told the operations sergeant not to do any favors; Ed would be booked on the next plane, due out the next morning. It impressed the hell out of the operations sergeant and the S3, but when I went to the trailer and told Ed, he didn't love me for it—but he understood.

Early the next morning, I took Ed to Bien Hoa myself then returned to the battalion for Mass. My chaplain was a Protestant, but on Sundays, a Catholic one would visit from Long Binh. That day I discovered that the chapel was located right next to the steam bath, a juxtaposition that I would never get used to.

I was sitting in the church when my driver came in and tapped me on the shoulder. We went outside where he could talk.

"Sir, you're wanted immediately at the Headquarters building. General McDowell is sitting in your office, sir."

General McDowell, a three-star general, was commander of all USARV. Needless to say, I made the trip from the chapel to Headquarters, a distance of a couple of hundred yards, quickly. Inside the building, several white-faced clerks pointed to my office. The general was sitting at my conference table, his baseball cap on the table, legs crossed, and looking up at me.

"I'm General McDowell. Let's have a briefing."

It raced through my mind that he must know that this was my first day in command of the battalion. Even though the office was air-conditioned, I could feel perspiration start running down my back. The only thing I could think of was to turn to the charts Ed had gone through rather rapidly and perfunctorily the day before. The General seemed to accept this, so I continued—giving him the breakdown of how many people had been shipped out in the last six months, as opposed to the same six months the prior year, and the rate of inbound people during the same time. He sat there passively, taking it all in.

When we reached the statistics about the PX, he asked, "Why have the receipts of the PX dropped so much in July?"

"Probably it has something to do with the number of people who passed through the battalion that month," I replied. I felt like an idiot. He didn't pursue the point. I went on wishing I had paid even closer attention to what Ed had been saying to me yesterday.

I finished the last chart.

"Sit down," said the general. "Where did you come from, and how long have you been in the service?"

These were typical new arrival pleasantries. I answered dutifully.

Then he leaned over—he was only inches from my face—and said, "Colonel Campbell, I have one piece of advice for you: Don't trust nobody, because I don't." With that, he got up and walked out. I followed him. I was wondering where his sedan was parked. He got into a jeep on the driver's side, and as he backed out, I noticed the canvas flap concealing his three-star plate on the front of the jeep. He turned on to the main road and headed off toward the back gate.

I was soaking wet. I went back inside and sat down with Fred and tried to figure out what was going on. I called Colonel Lewis and told him about General McDowell's visit. Lewis was shocked. He had heard no mention of the general's intention to visit the 90th Replacement Battalion.

After I'd gotten over my alarm, I tried to put together a daily routine. I sat down with Fred Meyers and we divided the workload. Fred and the adjutant would be responsible for all the administration. I didn't want to get involved with it. I called Captain Wills and told him that any supply problems should be brought to my immediate attention. Captain Holt and I discussed the operations of the battalion. I told him I would be available at any time. I also let the staff know that I wouldn't spend much time in Headquarters—I felt it was better spent out with the company commanders.

The next few days I spent touring the battalion area. I wanted to meet all the people in the battalion and get to know what facilities were available to the transients and how well they were operated. First, Captain Wills and I went to visit the motor pool. CWO Russo had been a wheeled vehicle warrant for about twenty years and knew his stuff. His motor pool was at the back end of the battalion, right at the gate. He had a staff of about ten or fifteen mechanics and drivers.

The battalion had forty-three vehicles, most of which had been in Vietnam since 1965. Many had belonged to another outfit and had been transferred to the 90th when it arrived in country. All the jeeps had more than 100,000 miles of use, so the biggest problem the motor pool had was the lack of spare parts. The only thing keeping the vehicles running was the fact that so many units were standing down and going home. But CWO Russo, much like CWO

Campbell, had an informal organization working throughout Vietnam and he knew where and when parts could be gotten — usually scrounged and brought back to the 90th. I was glad to see Mr. Russo working like a man possessed to keep his vehicles running, because without him, the battalion would have had difficulty performing its mission.

Right next to the motor pool was the Central Issue Facility (CIF). Its mission was to hand out all field gear except rifles: helmets, socks, shorts, t-shirts, jungle fatigues, and jungle boots. Usually on the morning after arrival, a replacement's first stop would be the CIF. The problem with the whole operation was that many sizes seemed perpetually out of stock. I was constantly being harangued by commanders of units who would get their replacements without a full complement of gear. The letters from those commanders went through USARV to my desk, something that irked me because they should have been going to the desk of the quartermaster who ran the depot that supplied the CIF.

The PX manager, Mr. Ono, had been in the Army Air Force Post Exchange System for over twenty years. He had a staff of about thirty Vietnamese women, and his building was small and always clean. Most important, though, it was well stocked with merchandise. If Mr. Ono didn't have it, the item was not to be found in Vietnam. His reputation was such that we struggled to keep people away who weren't entitled to our PX privileges. I would get calls from generals asking for special requests.

Next to the PX was a long, single-story building. It housed vendors who sold almost everything from men's suits to military patches. These vendors were either Vietnamese or businessmen from Japan, Thailand or Korea. Most transients who passed through the battalion would take at least one gift home from the shops. One particular vendor made a living on gift wrapping.

The 90th also had one of the infamous steam baths that were drawing all sorts of press coverage back in the States. Ours was the newest and most substantial building on the compound. It was made of whitewashed cinderblock and comprised a big, open lobby where there were a lot of rubdown tables and a large steam pool. On the other side were six or seven private stalls, which were for officers. Mr. Kim, a Korean, was the manager and owner. He had about twenty-five girls housed in the back. This was a place I checked on constantly because I didn't want my name in the news. I spelled it out plainly for Kim that if I ever caught his employees offering any extracurricular activities, I would close him down. Surprisingly enough, most of the people at church on Sundays were these very girls, as well as Vietnamese employees from the PX. Very few GIs ever showed up at church.

Directly across the street was a swimming pool. This, I was told, was the only in-ground American swimming pool in Vietnam. It was a popular place. The sign outside limited occupancy to a hundred people, but most times it was teeming, with even more men queued up outside. The specialist who ran the pool had his hands full, mostly in keeping law and order. The pool had a volleyball net at one end, and the games were as rough as any professional football game in the States.

Another difficulty he faced was getting chemicals. The medics periodically checked the water, and just as often, I'd receive memos about its dangerous levels of bacteria. The pool would then have to be drained.

Next was the snack bar, another enormous building. The fare included hot dogs, hamburgers, and soft drinks. I was interested in the kitchen's cleanliness. All the people working in the snack bar were Vietnamese contracted through the PX. One morning walking through the snack bar kitchen, a mama-san was squatting on the floor, cleaning pots. A huge water bug darted near her foot; she took off her sandal, snapped it down on the bug, picked up the bug, and flipped it in the oven. I stood, mesmerized. About four minutes later, she turned the oven off, took the now-crisp insect out, and proceeded to eat it. This event notwithstanding, the snack bar was run well and a favorite with the transients.

My other two points of concentration were the clubs. Both the officers' club and the NCO/EM club opened at nine in the morning and served liquor and beer until 9 p.m. In the early days of my tour, a Vietnamese group of four or five musicians had learned to play rock and roll, and their band played every night. They brought speakers the size of small refrigerators, and it was impossible to hear anything else. I closed down the NCO/EM club each night myself. This was the prime place for trouble to start, so I would always arrive fifteen minutes before closing time and stand or walk around and nod. Each night it was an effort. There was always someone—sometimes a group—who couldn't see any reason for the fun to end.

Another critical concern was the security of the compound's outer boundary. The entire area was surrounded by barbed wire. All but the portion facing Route 1 was internal wire which separated the 90th from other units. The front wire was guarded by five watchtowers, each manned continuously by people from the security platoon. The watchtowers were twenty feet off the ground, constructed of wood and reinforced on the outside by sandbags. They reminded me of the French lookout towers described in *Street Without Joy*. I made it a point to check them at least once during the day and twice at night. The night check was a disagreeable task for two reasons. First, even though we had lights illuminating the front wire, they weren't protected from the rain. They would short out, leaving you to feel your way along. Second, the two watchtowers on the north side were on the edge of a swamp. During the rainy season, I'd be up to my ankles in mud

Once I felt a little more comfortable about my surroundings, I decided it was time to visit Camp Alpha. My driver insisted on taking me down, rather than letting me drive myself. I relented because the road network in and around Tan Son Nhut had changed drastically in the last five years and I wasn't sure I could find my way.

Early one morning, we set out. Traffic was a mess. As the joke went, traffic was always exactly the same—terrible—because a lot of families lived in the same dwelling. If it wasn't your turn to sleep, you had to go out and ride a motor scooter around until someone got up and left space in the bed.

When we reached the outskirts of the city, traffic became especially intense. It was so close that you felt at any moment a motor scooter might punch through one side of the jeep and out the other. I had a habit of riding with my right leg cocked and my knee leaning out. A Vietnamese military truck buzzed so close that it hit the side-view mirror and bent it back into the cockpit. From then on, I kept my knee inside.

We finally arrived at Camp Alpha. I was surprised at how new it looked. It was a small compound with cinderblock buildings. The commander, Major Huff, greeted me and took me on a tour that started with breakfast. CWO Campbell's fine hand was evident at the mess hall. From there, we visited the processing center, a large one-story building. It consisted of a wide hallway flanked by offices. In the hall were classroom-style chairs—the kind with writing arms—where people going on R&R would fill out their paperwork. The whole place was orange and yellow and had music piped in over the sound system. What impressed me about Camp Alpha was the fact that it was a happy place. Most of the people there were going on R&R. There was a nicely appointed combination Officer/EM club, a PX, and an above-ground swimming pool. Another thing that impressed me about Alpha was the fact that the facilities were so new and modern. Maintenance problems were almost nil.

I spent most of the day with Major Huff, watching the processing. It was very efficient. People arrived, showered, changed and were booked out on the same day. Planes didn't go to all the R&R sites every day, but people were scheduled into Alpha on the day they were to actually depart. The camp PX did a huge business in slacks and sport shirts. Most of the people coming out of the field had no civilian clothes.

It was getting late and I decided I had better start back up Route 1. Just as we left, I remembered that the Vietnamese High Command was right around the corner. I told my driver to make a left, and I guided him right to the front door. We were stopped by the Vietnamese MPs who used mirrors to check under the jeep for bombs. They waved us through, and as we drove down the main street, one I had driven down hundreds of times in 1965 and 1966, the driver's eyes grew wide—he had never been around Vietnamese military before.

We passed the command headquarters and stopped at the Vietnamese data processing shop, where I had spent most of my time in the mid-1960s. We parked outside the compound and walked in. Things looked exactly the same as they had five years earlier. I was met by Lieutenant Colonel Ho, the officer who had taken command while I was the advisor. Ho was happy to see me. He had been a captain when I left five years earlier as a major, and I kiddingly told him he was doing better than I was.

He showed me around and took me very proudly into the computer room, which now housed an IBM 360 model 40. The Vietnamese were competent data processors. Most of the military people in the unit in 1965, and now in 1971, had been civilians trained by the French. In 1965, the same room had contained IBM punch card equipment. The computer printer seemed to be working overtime, spewing out different multi-colored forms. I asked Ho what he was printing. They were ballots for the forthcoming elections. I asked why they were using a computer printer and not the printing plant. Ho replied these were very important papers and couldn't be trusted to the printing press.

He brought me a cup of tea, and we sat and talked over old times. I had the highest respect for Colonel Ho. He had come out of the North during the exodus of 1954. He was a very intelligent, hard-working man, not only in military matters but in his community. He helped neighbors dig wells and improve their living conditions. If we had had more Colonel Hos in the Vietnamese

Army, Vietnam might not have fallen to the North.

When I got back to the battalion, I was pleasantly surprised to find an old friend waiting in my office.

"Sandy! How did you know I was the Commander?"

"Your picture in the 381st Company orderly room. You're as ugly as ever." Sandy was on his way home. He had commanded a signal battalion up in the highlands. I'd known him for years. We had served together in France some fifteen years earlier, where our families had become friendly. He and his family were devout, and he was an especially warmhearted, helpful person. Needless to say, I set him up in the front bedroom of my trailer.

The next evening we were sitting out on the patio, talking. In his serious way Sandy said, "Bill, you're just starting out with your command. There will be times you'll make a decision that in retrospect, when you sit down and think about it, will make you wonder how you did it—who helped you." He was intimating God was going to help me make critical decisions.

"That's ridiculous," I chuckled.

But many times, I thought of that conversation with Sandy, and how right he was. There were times when I did wonder who had helped me, because I wasn't smart enough or quick enough to have done so well. Unfortunately, after my return to the United States, I lost contact with Sandy, and have never been able to find him. We had exchanged Christmas cards for many years. His just stopped arriving and mine were returned stamped "undeliverable." I never had a chance to tell him how right he was.

After being in the country about a week, I began to review my job and the problems facing me. I felt more like the mayor of a small town than the commander of a unit. There were three mess halls, a snack bar, an officers' club, an NCO/EM club, a swimming pool, a steam bath, a PX, vendors, a chapel serving all denominations, a police force, a fire department, and a fleet of forty-three vehicles. When you added the facilities at Alpha, it was not a town—it was a city.

One area of concern was the constant turnover. We had a good staff, but maintaining such a high caliber workforce would take effort. Another concern was the age of the vehicles. Each one was well used, and we needed all of them all the time. Would they hold up for another year?

The condition of the buildings was also a problem. Because of the climate, they were aging rapidly and difficult to repair because there wasn't much lumber in the supply chain. The lumber issued each month was barely enough to keep up with the normal loss. I decided that my biggest worry during the forthcoming year would be a fire—but it wasn't my only worry. Most of our structures were infested either by termites or by carpenter ants, and others showed evidence of dry rot. The bottom boards in the kitchen of the 259th's mess hall no longer existed. One afternoon, we lost the paint shed in the motor pool—a gust of wind during a rain storm simply blew it over. An inspection revealed that the supporting beams had been eaten completely through.

Little did I know what my real problems were to be.

CHAPTER 3
GOLD FLOW PLANNING

During my daily tours around the battalion, I was making it a point not only to observe the soldiers entering the battalion after a year in Vietnam, but also to talk to them. For the most part, they were hostile. The talk centered around their absolute hate for Vietnam, the war, and the Army. They all knew—to the hour—how many days they had left in country and in the Army.

Some of the returnees seemed different. I had never been exposed to drug users, and I really didn't know what to expect. I knew a druggie wouldn't be wearing a sign around his neck. But after a few days there *were* signs that were almost as unmistakable. Some of the soldiers were extremely nervous. Others were carefree and happy; others simply stared. Almost everyone stationed in Vietnam lost a lot of weight. The most serious cases among the drug users, however, were visibly emaciated. Their uniforms hung on them and were in a state of filth and disrepair.

I really didn't expect an admission of guilt, but I was hoping that someone would share stories. Not one soldier opened up to me. The worst cases were usually pugnacious and showed little respect for anyone or anything. These were the potential powder kegs. They could cause a confrontation at any time or place if they thought someone was "fucking them over," as they put it. The problem with a fight was that it could erupt into a full-fledged race riot. Racial tension was always on or just beneath the surface of every situation. Blacks hung around with blacks, and whites with whites. Seldom did you see a black soldier and a white soldier together.

The Chief of Chaplains, USARV, visited the battalion. I had met him briefly in Hawaii.

"Welcome to the country and battalion," he said. "I'll do anything I can to help." I brought up the topic of drugs and mentioned my observations. His surprised look took me aback.

"There's not much abuse," he said. "The troopers are using pot to some degree, but not many are using heroin. In fact, the Army is successful in countering the abuse of drugs. We have rehabilitation centers established throughout Vietnam, in fact, eleven of them in operation at this time."

I had been exposed somewhat to this voluntary program in Hawaii. I felt these halfway houses met with little success. Many soldiers were reluctant to identify themselves as drug users, and were suspicious of the treatment they would receive if they did. Like the Chief of Chaplains, I used to think the primary drug problem was marijuana, not heroin. But my daily walks through the battalion, stepping on endless numbers of empty vials, led me to believe heroin was the true enemy. When I pursued the subject, the Chief of Chaplains changed the topic to—of all things—the new retreat house being built at Cam Rhan Bay, a project of which he was very proud. I thought, "My God, are we planning to stay forever in this country? Why would we be building retreat houses?"

No amount of prodding could get him back to the subject of drugs.

At a later date, I visited Cam Rhan Bay for a change of command ceremony. The Chaplain had been true to his word— the retreat house was beautiful and resembled a Swiss chalet.

Other officers at USARV felt that heroin use was on the rise among the soldiers, but no one would guess what percentage of the people were using it. There was general agreement that the voluntary drug rehabilitation centers were not the answer. In fact, most felt these were nothing but drug warehouses.

That afternoon Colonel Lewis called me to say I was to attend a briefing at USARV that evening. When I asked what it was about, he said the subject was classified.

On my way to USARV Headquarters that afternoon, I drove my own jeep. I didn't know how long the briefing might last and I didn't want the driver to hang around. On the trip I discovered what an unstable vehicle the jeep really is. Driving down a roadway coated with oil to keep down the dust, I came to an intersection where I had to negotiate a turn. I was going less than ten miles per hour when I cut the steering wheel. Halfway through the maneuver, the two outside wheels left the ground. I felt the jeep beginning to roll to the left. It would be only a matter of moments before it would go completely over on its side. As I tried to throw my body weight to the right, the balance shifted and the two right tires returned to the road. I steered to the shoulder, stopped the jeep, and got out to have a cigarette.

I entered the briefing room with Colonels Lewis and Gardner. There were only three other lieutenant colonels in the room: Commander of the MP Battalion, Ed Murphy; the Medical Battalion Commander, John O'Day; and the Commander of the Engineer Battalion, Jake Largent. While we waited for the meeting to start, we tried to guess what we might be about to hear. The most lighthearted and most hoped-for conjecture was that we might be totally out of country by July 4th.

It wasn't to be. General Martin, DCSPER, and General Kelley, DCSLOG, entered the room. They were accompanied by Brigadier General Meyer, Chief Surgeon, and two civilians. General Kelley took the podium and snapped on the light behind a red sign reading SECRET. General Kelley introduced the two civilians who were from Washington and would give the briefing. The subject was to be the President's campaign against drug abuse in Vietnam.

It came to me that while the drug problem was not officially defined, there were people working on the solution. I came to the conclusion that previously, the use of drugs had been attacked on a voluntary basis because nobody had yet worked out a solution to the problem.

One of the civilians stepped to the podium. He informed the audience that President Nixon was about to declare war on drug addicts and traffickers. The President would announce in a few short days the Special Action Office for Drug Abuse Prevention (SAODAP) in the White House. The director would be Dr. Jerome Jaffe. Initially, the presentation glossed over the effects of drugs on a person. He reviewed the different types in use, but centered his attention on pot and heroin, pointing out how lethal heroin can be. The difficulty in uncovering drug users in the past had been the lack of a practical method of detection. Chemically, urinalysis could reveal heroin or marijuana use, but the process was time-consuming and impractical for a large-scale program.

Now, a machine had been developed which could process hundreds of urine samples per hour. It was referred to as the Free Radical Assay Technique (FRAT). The briefer showed slides of how the result of a urine sample by this machine would indicate not only the degree of heroin abuse, but also caffeine and nicotine. If they ever start checking for nicotine abusers, I thought, Colonel Lewis is in trouble. Indeed, at that moment he asked to borrow another cigarette.

The machine was exact and could be calibrated to register degrees of use, from very mild to very heavy. However, each sample the FRAT uncovered as positive would also be run through two additional chemical tests to ensure accuracy. The critical threshold between the occasional and the serious user would be fixed by medical personnel. The exact threshold, however, would never be revealed to the other military personnel working in the program. But by January 1972, the two additional chemical tests would be discontinued, because FRAT proved to be a sufficient indicator of use.

Everyone leaving country and returning permanently to the United States would be subject to urinalysis. If a soldier tested positive, he would be held in country and detoxified. His detoxification period would end after seven days or when he had successfully given two consecutive urine tests with negative results. Then and only then would he be allowed to re-process through the replacement battalion and go home.

The civilian presenter pointed out that the Nixon administration was asking Congress to enact a law to allow mandatory extension of service obligations for those found to be addicts and to allow mandatory detoxification in the Veterans Administration hospitals stateside. Interestingly enough, Congress never did enact the legislation to extend the addicts' length of service, or make provisions for mandatory detoxification. The VA hospitals were, however, opened to the returning veteran on a voluntary basis, but a 1974 study by SAODAP indicated that only 4 percent of those found positive at DEROS used this option.

Currently, uncertainty about drug use prevailed. One theory held that use of lesser drugs automatically led to use of heavier drugs. According to the briefer, the heroin habit was difficult to kick. The Army was about to embark on the biggest crusade against drug users ever attempted. The program was given the code name Gold Flow.

After the civilians completed the briefing, which ran longer than expected because of the audience's questions, Generals Kelley and Martin took the floor.

"The program must be kept secret," Kelley explained. "All your planning efforts must be done with the minimum number of people. The program will be announced by the publication and reading of a short Presidential announcement."

Everyone leaving Vietnam and returning to the United States on permanent change of station orders would give a urine sample: both sexes, all grades and ranks, no exceptions allowed. Medical personnel would watch the sample being taken. The program would be conducted in the two replacement battalions, north and south. No one would be booked on an aircraft until his urine sample was negative. Those whose samples were positive would be pulled out of the replacement battalion and sent to the detoxification center. Upon clearing the detoxification center, the person would be returned to the replacement battalion for out-processing to the United States.

Since the battalion commander of the 22nd Replacement Battalion was not present, the question of the detox center's location directed at General Kelley was for the Long Binh area only. He said it would be set up in the old transportation area just outside the back gate of the 90th. (I heard a big sigh from the Engineer Lieutenant Colonel; the area had been unoccupied for some time and was in very poor shape.) The center would be manned by medical personnel and military police: the medics to assist the soldiers going through withdrawal and the MPs to prevent trouble. No one who didn't belong would be allowed in or out of the center. This was to prevent drug trafficking.

From this time on, the replacement battalion was to be closed to outsiders. No one could go in or out without approval, a move that made both my security platoon leader and me happy. Because Mr. Ono ran the best PX in Vietnam and always had a good stock of desirable items, like cameras and stereo equipment, many of the USARV staff officers would come down to do their shopping. I always felt they were taking the prime merchandise away from the transients and from members of the 90th. The rule would also give us some clout to keep assignment personnel from coming in to take their inbound buddies out for a night.

The lieutenant colonel from the medics asked where he would get the extra medical personnel to run the machine and serve as observers. He was told that they were at that very moment being selected in the States for ninety-day temporary duty in Vietnam. The obvious question followed: Is this only a ninety-day program? No. But the extra medics are needed to get it off the ground. The medics will be replaced with permanent staff at the end of the program's initiation period. There would be some unhappy medical people in the States tonight, I thought. Some had probably just left Vietnam a few months before and would have to do an about face.

My head was reeling. The Univac 1005 program would have to be changed. Here was yet another thing the GIs had to do before being booked, one more step that could fall prey to Murphy's Law. And what would we do with the belongings of people who were going to the detox center?

At that moment I was brought back by General Martin's closing comment: "Gentlemen, the program will commence at 0600 hours on 15 June." I looked at the date through the scratched crystal of my watch: 10 June. "Are there any questions? No? Thank you, gentlemen. Good luck."

The four lieutenant colonels looked around at one another. They had a million questions, but the problem was where to start asking. Colonels Gardner and Lewis departed, assuring me I had their utmost support if I needed anything. That left four very bewildered lieutenant colonels in the room.

Someone said, "Typical Army! Great idea, but as it passed through each level of staff, from DA to USARV, everyone yessed the President or Commander. Sure, two weeks! Next level, can do! One week! Some superman staff guy says five days. Of course he is no way involved with the solution to the problem. Shit!"

The suggestion was made to go to the club and get a steak. Because we couldn't talk about the subject in the club, we could at least take our minds off things while we ate. We went to the club, but I know my mind was never once distracted, and I am sure I was not the only one, since there wasn't much talking.

Afterwards we all drove to the 90th and went straight to my office. I knew we were in for a long go, and I was concerned that we could not pull the entire operation together in a matter of four days. But at that moment I didn't realize that I had seen my bed for the last time for a while.

Most of the night was spent making a list of what had to be done—a list that posed more questions than answers. There were two underlying problems we could not solve. Both were crucial to the planning of the operation. The first involved our soldiers' reaction. Would they rebel? Based on the low morale and disgruntlement I had witnessed, this seemed like a real danger. The second was closely linked to the first. How many drug users would we have on our hands? Our guesses ranged from two to twenty percent. Twenty percent would present a serious discipline problem, both in the 90th and at the detox center. And we might face extreme overcrowding in the center. We settled on ten percent as a working figure: with 250,000 men in Vietnam, minus the 70,000 officers, we calculated that ten percent would give us 18,000 men over fifty-two weeks, or 350 men per week split between two replacement battalions, therefore, about 175 men per week. But there was no real data.

Someone said, "There sure isn't any book or regulation on this subject."

"Shut up!" another one of us shot back. "We four are writing the book. You're the one who's behind in production of chapters."

The Engineer Lieutenant Colonel, Jake Largent, had a tough assignment: putting the transportation area back together. The buildings were only shells. He had to assemble a mess hall and place a chain-link fence with a barbed wire top around the entire compound. He had to turn a maintenance set-up with bays and tool sheds into a legitimate medical facility. Moreover, he had to design and build a latrine in which people could be observed while giving their samples—a different twist.

I decided to do a complete shakedown of all returnees, including all their baggage. This would be time consuming and cause a backup of people at the front gate. So in addition to the covered shed where the shakedown would take place, I wanted a covered runway leading to it to keep the waiting soldiers out of the sun and rain.

Jake said, "This item isn't first on my priority list."

I agreed it shouldn't be. "Just give me the lumber and I'll have my people build it." I had two good carpenters, who up until this time had tried just holding the place together. Jake gladly agreed to the arrangement.

The medic and I had other problems to solve: how to ensure a batch of urine would not get put aside and other soldiers would be cleared while those who went before them cooled their heels.

That would be inviting rebellion. What kind of vehicle would move the samples the two miles to the laboratory where the FRAT was set up? We chose an ambulance because the door could be secured. The urine could not be tampered with while being carried to the laboratory.

Ed Murphy, the MP, and I had procedures to work out as well. How would we transport the positives to the detox center? What would we do with these soldiers' belongings? Ed was responsible for processing all returnees through his customs agents prior to boarding the plane, which presented a difficulty—each returnee began his trip in the customs shed, a big building with low tables running parallel throughout, and on one of these tables, he would place his baggage for a customs MP to go through. The baggage was held for the returnee in a secure area, loaded by the 90th people, and trucked to the plane. The soldier couldn't get back into his baggage until he claimed it in the United States. So, if the soldier happened to test positive before leaving, we would have to make some arrangement for keeping his belongings from leaving Vietnam without him. We'd also have to figure out whether it made sense to send detainees to the customs shed before they entered detox or after their release.

I didn't want to put those who tested positive through customs prior to going to the detoxification center for a couple of reasons. First, it would delay getting them out of the battalion, and given time, anyone could leave the 90th without too much difficulty. Second, I did not have the space to store all those belongings securely. Ed, on the other hand, wanted to put the positives through customs at the 90th. this would preclude his requiring additional customs MPs at the detox center. If storage was required at detox, we'd both have to let Jake know right away, because he would then have to alter his building plans at the detox center. Ed finally capitulated. Jake would have to build a secure area where the baggage would be housed at detox.

The other issue between us was that I wanted Ed to provide some of his MPs for the initial day of testing. He argued that if MPs were visible around the battalion that day, it could trigger problems. He wanted no part of it. In hindsight, his resistance seems sound—but on the night of June 10th, 1971, it didn't seem that way. He also told me to keep my MPs out of sight as well. And whenever Ed said, "the 90th's MPs," he almost choked on the words. He didn't look upon them as MPs because they were not school trained, and he kept making overtures to get my men assigned to him so that he would have full responsibility for law and order within the 90th. This I would fight throughout my tour, and Ed was never able to get a sympathetic ear from among the higher-ups.

Since Jake informed me that the latrine would not be completed by the kick-off day, he and I discussed the best alternative. It should be a location between the 381st and 259th Replacement Companies (for officers and enlisted, respectively), so that people wouldn't have a long trek. The deserted helicopter pad in the swamp area was the only conceivable place—but it was connected to the roadway by only a small footpath. The pad was constructed of sandbags covered by rubber matting, and had been off limits for a couple of years because it was in the flight path of helicopters landing at the tactical headquarters located next door. We had used it for "touch" football games (which were, in fact, brutal).

My concern was the pathway. It was old, and during the rainy season, the usual trickle beside it became a river. With150 GIs walking over the path each day, the fragile path might give way. Jake estimated that it would have to last a week to ten days, the time he needed to construct the latrine. We agreed to place a layer of crushed rock on the footpath in hopes this would give enough temporary support.

This and similar discussions went on throughout the night. It surprised us all when the sky began to lighten. I offered to buy breakfast for all, but everyone was too anxious. We each needed to return to our respective units to begin to set things in motion. As the three colonels passed through my Headquarters building to get to their jeeps, I could see all my troopers waiting to find out what was up.

"Fred, get the S-1, S-3, S-4, and the commanders of the 259th, 381st, and Headquarters Company together in my office in about an hour. Then call Bill Huff at Camp Alpha and get him up to Headquarters this afternoon."

After a shower, change of uniform and some breakfast, I briefed the staff on what was about to happen. To Captain Enright, my Adjutant, I said, "Contact Lewis to get reporting procedures squared away." In a war where numbers were a way of life—body counts were just one example—we would be required to report all sorts of statistics to Headquarters. "And since the program is still classified, you should speak to Lewis to find out whom you can deal with at the USARV level."

The discussions with the S-4 centered around the shakedown area the carpenters were building at the front gate. I told Enright to come up with some plans for the size and location of the area. Both of us should take a look at the proposed spot that afternoon. We also discussed the interim urine collection site on the helicopter pad. I told him about the request for crushed rock on the path leading from the road to the pad and asked him to follow up with his counterpart in the engineer battalion.

The company commander at Headquarters, Joe Stanley, was interested in the shakedown point because his MPs would have to man it. He offered a few suggestions on what it should look like, but his main concern was staffing. I told him and the adjutant that Lewis's assignment people were to divert about ten newly arriving MPs to us. Knowing Joe's passion for doing a good job, I felt confident he would badger Captain Enright until he got the new people.

I made it a point to impress upon Joe that the shakedown was to be very thorough. I wanted all weapons, including illegal knives. One rule—an Army regulation—was that a man could have a knife no longer than two and one half inches. Many GIs, however, had armed themselves with much more lethal ones. I couldn't blame them for doing so, but they were not allowed to be processed through to the States with weapons. With such tight security, we would also have a chance to clean up the flow of drugs into the compound. My fondest dream was to do away with those empty plastic vials that littered the area. Joe fully understood, and I was confident his shakedown would be tight.

I then asked my company commanders for their best guess on how many drug users we would uncover. Their estimate was higher than the battalion commanders', and I respected their judgment. They knew the soldiers on a more intimate level, and they were more concerned about the reaction to the program. Some said, "You'll have trouble. The first person to balk will have to be handled quickly and harshly. Send him back immediately to his unit and make sure the word is spread."

"How many officers might test positively?" I asked. The 381st Company commander, Gerry White, thought that there would be only a few younger officers picked up.

The discussion with the two other company commanders and the operations officer moved on to discuss where to build the permanent urine collection point and what the procedures would be. "We'll get back to you this afternoon," they said. "Remember, the project's classification is 'secret,'" I warned.

Keeping it that way was more of a problem than it might seem. The one thing a GI is not, is a fool. He will usually discern what's going on without being told. The men of the 90th were going to have to be gotten around somehow. We decided to say the front gate construction was to keep troopers out of the weather. But no one could come up with a good cover for the construction of latrine pits on the helicopter pad.

Captain Wills and I went up to the front gate with the two carpenters to design the shakedown point and the runway leading to it. Four shakedown tables would fit without readjusting the barbed wire. After an hour or so, we had a rough drawing of what was needed. The two GIs were surprisingly good carpenters and never once asked for an explanation. Captain Wills and I discussed building an amnesty box and placing it on the runway. I felt we'd need a big one. The soldiers would hopefully offload anything they thought might keep them from going home.

We worked up a rough cut of the wording for a sign:

DRUGS – WEAPONS – GOVERNMENT PROPERTY
THIS IS YOUR LAST CHANCE

Not in my wildest dreams did I imagine what we were soon to gather from that box.

Bill Huff, the CO of Alpha, arrived that afternoon. John Holt and I filled him in on the details of the program. Huff felt that he would pick up very few positives, since most of his returnees were MACV advisors, primarily officers, and NCOs. His difficulties lay in selecting latrine facilities, transporting the samples to Long Binh, and getting the results back fast enough so that his work didn't create a bottleneck in the larger screening process. Delays, of course, would mean empty seats on the airplanes. His returning population was small compared to the 90th at Long Binh. Most of his soldiers were troopers going on R&R, and they were not required to present a sample.

That evening the four battalion commanders met at the 90th to review our progress. Throughout the day, I had noticed truckloads of material and men on the way to the old transportation area. I reminded Jake how long he had been unable to provide me with any lumber.

"Keep your guys away from it," he ordered.

Summoning my best look of outraged innocence, I said, "Who me? I would never appropriate any of your lumber."

"I've set up lights," he stated, "and I'll be working around the clock, making it impossible for you to get at the material." He added, "I'll start the footings on the latrine tomorrow. But I'll have no carpenters to spare until next week." That meant the helicopter pad would have to do for at least a week, as we figured. The lumber for the shakedown point would arrive tomorrow, the gravel the next day.

John O'Day reported that the FRAT machine had been set up and that the medics from the States would begin to arrive in a couple of days. The staff of doctors for the detox center would begin arriving tomorrow.

Ed Murphy and I had a serious discussion about his support. He was sticking to his guns.

"The MP presence will cause more problems than they will prevent. But I will have my people on call close by." Because none of us could predict the response to the program, I was becoming more and more concerned as the deadline neared. The program's start, of course, was going to be a complete surprise to the soldiers. I had some experience with what happened when a person, for some reason, was overlooked or was processed out of turn to the States. One syndrome of a transient was that immediately upon entering the 90th, he would stop thinking of anything except home—so much so that some men would actually miss the bus to the airport at Bien Hoa. But if the delay was our fault, the mistake always came to my attention in a most vociferous manner. I was envisioning the worst of scenarios.

The meeting went through the night. We proposed to meet with all our staffs at the 90th the next evening to update each other and review any problems.

I had been so wrapped up in the project that my normal tours of the battalion area had not taken place for a couple of days. Fred assured me all was okay, but I decided I needed the exercise and walked around. Fred was true to his word. The population was down to about an average of 400 per night. There was a slow trickle of returnees. I only hoped that the low volume would continue until we had a chance to try the program out. It would be so much easier.

My staff met with me later the next morning. Adjutant Enright had set up his reporting procedures. The medics would report up through their command chain, and we would report up the personnel chain. The number of positives would be listed by grade and unit in racial groupings.

"In all probability," Enright said, "the USARV computer group will be given the mission of reducing this data and establishing a program to report the figures to the Department of the Army." That meant my old buddy, Charlie, would be up to his ears in the program. It crossed my mind that Charlie would be coming through the front door any day now.

The S-4 reported that the carpenters were pleased and eager to start work on the shakedown point. He figured the mess hall would be repaired in short order, too. The carpenters wanted to get CWO Campbell off their asses. George chimed in that he would have the latrine holes on the helicopter pad dug by the end of the day. John Holt said the programming changes to process the data on our UNIVAC were being worked on by Sergeant Whitehead. He recommended the urine collection point be next to the 259th's processing point. That meant that officers would have to walk down to the enlisted area to give a sample, but had the advantage of allowing the processing NCOs to group the enlisted men—who made up most of the population—and just walk them a few yards to begin their processing. I agreed with John's logic and gave Jake the go-ahead.

Bill Huff at Alpha designated a collection latrine which he felt two medics could observe without a problem. Twice a day he shipped samples in closed, locked cases on the courier vehicle.

During the evening meeting in my office, Fred came in and said a Major Leavit from the USARV Criminal Investigation Unit had to see me immediately. He wouldn't take no for an answer. I stepped out of my office into Fred's. Major Leavit was an MP officer I had known in Hawaii. In fact, he used to live right down the street. Tonight, he looked very glum.

"What can I do for you?" I asked. I expected it would have something to do with the drug program. His next words stunned me.

"I'm here to investigate you."

Fred and I looked at one another. Major Leavit added, "General McDowell visited the battalion yesterday. During his visit he entered the steam bath and found beer on the premises, strictly against the rules."

I said, "That's impossible. Mr. Kim knows better. He would lose his contract with the Army if he violated the regulation."

"But General McDowell's aide was the person who spotted the beer," Leavit claimed. "At the general's request he wrote the memo asking for a full investigation."

"Damn it!" I snapped. "Okay, Fred, you and Leavit get on with the investigation. I have to go back inside."

The meeting lasted all night once again. Jake was working his troopers into the ground trying to get the detox center ready. Everything seemed to be falling into place. For the first time, I began to feel that we were going to pull it off. But I was still worried about the reaction when the surprise was sprung. It was obvious to me that everyone assigned to the 90th knew what was coming, but among the transients, there seemed to be a total lack of interest.

I had completely forgotten about Major Leavit and the steam bath when he came in and said he had gotten the full story.

"The 18th Replacement Company's first sergeant is a Hawaiian."

"What's that got to do with beer in the steam bath?" I scoffed.

Leavit looked at me. "Hold on, Colonel, and hear me out. Yesterday was Sunday."

"It was?" I had forgotten to go to church. Another sharp look from Leavit.

"There's a Hawaiian group at Long Binh, and yesterday there was a luau. Your first sergeant was responsible for collecting and bringing the beer to the party. After loading about twelve cases into his jeep, he started out of the battalion. The jeep broke down right in front of the steam bath. He knew if he left the beer unattended while he went back to the motor pool, it would be gone when he got back. So he off-loaded it into the steam bath and asked Mr. Kim to watch it while he was gone. When General McDowell and his aide toured the steam bath, according to Mr. Kim, it was the aide who spotted it behind the opened front door. I've spoken to Mr. Kim and the first sergeant separately, and their stories coincide. But Mr. Kim is quite upset and he'll probably be in to see you soon."

"What's the next step?"

"I'll write the incident up and forward the account to my boss." I felt both relieved and nervous. The story sounded a bit thin. Would General McDowell buy it?

As Leavit had predicted, Mr. Kim arrived about an hour later, very concerned and assuring me things had happened just as Leavit said. "The General was very stern with me Sunday." I knew General McDowell didn't care for the steam baths, but he was stuck with them. I assured Mr. Kim everything would be all right. I wasn't so sure about me. Battalion commanders had been done in by even more ridiculous snafus. But what could General McDowell do to me, I thought—send me to Vietnam? Then the vision of those offices at USARV Headquarters came to mind. He could put me behind one of those desks, and that would be tough to take.

The next day was the 13th of June. I received a call from General Martin, a surprise. Ordinarily communications from him came through Lewis or Gardner. What he had to say shook me to my boots. The drug testing program would have to begin the next morning—not on the 15th as planned.

Calmly he told me, "At a news conference in Saigon, the chief medical officer made a mistake in dates. The 22nd Replacement Battalion at Cam Rhan Bay will kick off on the 15th as scheduled. The program will kick off here at the 90th tomorrow." What the hell, I thought, was he doing talking about it at all—especially to the press? I thought it was a military secret. General Martin continued, "General Kelley is informing Jake and John, and the provost marshal will inform Ed Murphy. Do you have any questions?"

I was too undone to think of any.

Immediately after I hung up the phone, it began to ring. The first caller was John—absolutely beside himself. The first minute of his conversation was impressively profane. His major problem was still the detox center. The medics weren't due in until late tonight. That meant he would have to put them to work immediately—men who had but one or two days to put their affairs in order before heading off to Vietnam. He asked me to get them directly to him rather than process them through the 90th's usual procedures. I assured him I would.

I called in my staff to give them the news. While we were discussing this new development, my sergeant major came in.

"Did you order a bulldozer into the swamp?"

I jumped to my feet. Out the window I could see the bulldozer sitting in an area just short of the helicopter pad. In the background was the darkest cloud I had ever seen. I ran out the building and raced a jeep toward the machine. The cloud was now directly overhead, and the sky opened up. I scarcely noticed the downpour and began to walk out across the path to where the bulldozer was mired. Its treads were lost in mud. A lone figure was standing atop the machine.

As I got closer I began to sink, too. The mud was up to my knees. I wanted to kill the man on the bulldozer. With great difficulty I slogged up to it and tried to pull myself up. The person made a move to help, but I waved him back. He was a first lieutenant and the name on his tag was Campbell. Fighting an instinct to throttle him, I asked what the hell he thought he was doing. By this time, the rain was so intense that to communicate we had to yell at each other. I could feel the water running down my back. He said he had just wanted to smooth the path before putting the rock on it. I goggled around—the truck with the rock had not even arrived yet.

My next communication was slow and loud.

"Lieutenant. Tomorrow at 0730 hours, I will walk about two hundred people over this path. You are to get this goddam contraption out of here, fill in the hole with big rock, and cover the path with smaller rock. If you do not have it done by 0730 tomorrow, I will personally assure you that you'll stay in Vietnam another six months after you are due to rotate."

He grew pale. "Yes, sir! Yes, sir!"

"Do you understand?"

"Yes, sir!"

With that I turned to leave. I was now faced with the problem of effecting a dignified retreat. I eased down off the bulldozer into the mud. Every step was an effort. I had to pull each leg out with my hands before taking a step. Finally, I reached fairly firm ground. The mud had caked on the bottom of my boots and run down inside them, and walking was difficult. I felt like an ungainly bird with weights on each foot. When I reached the road, I tried to scrape as much mud off the bottoms as I could to be able to drive.

That's when I realized that the sergeant major had followed me from the office and was still sitting in his jeep. He had not yet gotten out. He was more interested in keeping dry. I called to him and motioned him over. He seemed surprised and hesitated getting out of the jeep.

I called, "Now, Sergeant Major!"

It was still raining, but not quite as hard as before. When he arrived, I asked him what chance he thought we had of using the pad tomorrow. He assured me little or none. I said fine and that it was his job to see that we had alternate facilities available by 0730 tomorrow and that he had better talk with Captain Wills.

I got into the jeep, turned it around and headed for my trailer to change clothes. As I drove, I knew I was not going to sign the sergeant major's request for an extension—another six months in Vietnam—which at that moment was lying in my box. I always felt that anyone who extended had something going on the side that was either illegal or immoral. I would call Jack Dickey to start a search for a new sergeant major for the 90th.

The mama-san who maintained our quarters was in the area when I arrived. She demanded that I take my pants and boots off before entering the trailer. She was not going to clean up big gobs of mud. I didn't blame her.

The shower and clean uniform and boots felt good, but I didn't. I was really concerned about Lieutenant Campbell's ability to pull off my orders. At Headquarters, I called Jake and told him what had happened. I guess I was a little testy with him because he began to argue. Neither of us had any sleep in days. But the end of the conversation the phone took the brunt of my frustration.

"Fred, get the officers and NCOs of the enlisted and officer companies together in the newbie processing shack at 1800 hours. We will brief them concerning tomorrow."

I then called Huff at Camp Alpha. He was set to go. He had received a copy of the President's message, which he would read at first formation.

As people passed in and out of the office throughout the afternoon, I kept looking out the window to see the progress the lieutenant was making in the swamp. He had extracted the bulldozer from the mud using a tank retriever. (Later I often wondered where he laid his hands on it, but I never asked. Let it be his secret.) Trucks began to arrive with the rocks he would use to fill the gap caused by the dozer. The frantic pace of his work must have aged him ten years in a day.

At 1800 hours the people from the 259th and 381st Companies were assembled in the processing shack. I briefed them on the program. Most seemed aware of what was to happen the next morning. I read the President's message to them and gave out copies. I told them I would read the message again at the first formation in the 259th, and Gerry White would read it to the officers simultaneously. The NCOs were told that at future morning formations, the names of the positives would be read aloud, and those men would be instructed to collect their personal belongings and muster outside the Headquarters building of the 259th, from which they would be transported to the detox center.

I answered the usual question about the troops' reaction in the same manner I had for the three previous days. One of the processing sergeants recommended that all the NCOs from the 259th be present for the morning formation and be arrayed around the podium. The NCOs were concerned about violence. After much conversation, it was agreed that all NCOs would make the first formation and that bunk adapters would be hidden inside the podium—the round metal poles used to support one army bunk over another. It could also be used as a weapon.

Meanwhile, the shakedown point at the front gate was almost ready. The walls were rising rapidly around the tables. The new amnesty box with its last-chance sign was in place. Latrines on the pad were ready for use and we had been informed that medics would man their observation stations in the morning.

When I went by to check on Lieutenant Campbell, I assumed my sternest look. At first, he avoided catching my eye. When he finally did, he wanted to smile because both he and I knew the job would be done, but I gave him no chance. I don't believe I have ever been so angry with an officer before or since, but I must give Campbell credit. He got his act together and pulled off the job. He returned to his work still covered with mud; surely he wanted to finish and never lay eyes on me again.

The four battalion commanders gathered for a last meeting that evening. John O'Day's principal worry was putting medics directly to work off the plane from the States. He had worked out a plan to rotate people frequently to give each some sack time. Jake was dead on his feet, but the detox center was ready. The fence was not completed, but he had the ward set up and a mess hall operating. Of course, the lack of a fence put a bigger burden on Ed Murphy for security. He said his MPs would be on call, and he would be in my office personally at 0700 hours tomorrow. I reported my plans. We were as ready as we could be.

They departed at 2000 hours, and I immediately felt terrible. The coffee I had over the past three days had pickled my stomach in acid. I was so tired I could barely walk in a straight line. I staggered from the Headquarters building, thinking only of my trailer.

As I entered the compound, the head special services woman was leaving. Mary Laffin was a young, good-natured gal who had no interest in making the service a career. She had joined the special services to see the war firsthand, so I kidded her that the only reason she joined was to find a husband. She would always tell me to "bug off." Now, she looked at me with astonishment and asked when I had last eaten. I couldn't remember. When had I slept last? Three nights ago.

I thought, *why do most women sound like my mother?*

She sat me down at one of the tables and disappeared. About fifteen minutes later I was eating a steak she had hoarded. My manners took a back seat to my hunger, and I was glad no one was watching.

Before I went to bed, my last act was to call the charge of quarters and ask to be called on the field phone at 0500 hours. If I didn't answer, the CQ was to come to the trailer personally and wake me up.

CHAPTER 4
GOLD FLOW BEGINS

The field phone next to my bed buzzed at 0500. I fumbled for it. It was the CQ. I threw my legs over the side of the bed, realizing that if I didn't get up immediately, I would probably pass out again.

At the Headquarters building I met with my S-3, John Holt. We had a break. The day's returnee population was small. There were about 380 people waiting for processing. A plane was due out that afternoon which would have to be full. Otherwise, we had a remaining 150 or so who would be the first to undergo urine analysis—our first customers.

The company commanders of the 259th and the 381st came to my office for a final run-through. We would start the day like any other. The enlisted men would be assembled for police call, then the NCO would call out the plane manifest and turn the podium over to me for the reading of the President's proclamation.

I gave Captain White of the 381st a copy to read to the officers. According to the manifest, there would be only a handful of officers left to give samples. A call to Bill Huff confirmed that all was ready at Camp Alpha. He did not have a plane leaving that day from Saigon, so his entire population, a couple of hundred, would give samples. Joe Stanley had his MPs in position at the front gate to begin the shakedown process. The security platoon leader and a few MPs would be in place by 0700 in the battalion headquarters building directly across from the 259th, just in case the returnees got out of hand.

It was time to go live with Gold Flow. It was June 15th, 1971.

At 0700 hours the returnees were collected under the shed, knowing nothing about what they would face

The NCOs of the 259th took them through the area for police call. There were the usual remarks about going home, fuck the army, and Vietnam. At 0730 the troopers formed up. This was the easiest part because everyone wanted to be on that plane. The NCO began to call out the names for the afternoon flight. As each name was called, a soldier would leave the formation to gather his possessions and go to the customs shed. While the NCO was reading the list, the rest of the NCOs from the 259th were drifting into the area and taking up positions in and around the podium. As the last name was called, the troopers began to break up. The NCO called them back and announced that the battalion commander had an announcement to make.

I stepped up to the podium.

"I have a message from the President of the United States."

That didn't seem to impress them at all.

I read the directive. It was general in nature but specified that each person leaving Vietnam would have to give a urine sample. The initial reaction was dead silence. Then came questions.

"How long will this delay my departure?" someone called out.

I answered, "If negative, not at all. If positive, detoxification will last approximately seven days."

"Is this program for officers, also?"

"Yes."

There were some snide remarks about the officers.

The NCO marched them to the helicopter pad, where the medics were ready to begin taking samples. The first group took about an hour to give their specimens. So far, so good.

At the front gate, returnees were beginning to arrive in small groups. But because of our inexperience, the process was slow and created a backup. Joe Stanley had begun with only two of the four shakedown positions for the early morning. He opened the other two to get things moving.

Interestingly, the MPs were not picking up any contraband. Joe and I were both surprised. We should at least be getting knives. But by midmorning, an MP walked out of the shakedown shed to straighten up the line of soldiers outside on the road. As he walked by the amnesty box, he noticed it was overflowing.

The contents were taken to the S-3's office. The inventory included every conceivable sort of knife, water pipes of different sizes and shapes, and all sorts of medical supplies. But the most surprising discovery were the many pairs of surgical scissors. At first none of the officers or NCOs could figure out why there were so many. A young PFC from the battalion staff finally clued us in. The scissors were used to hold a roach to the last drag—to keep from burning one's fingers. From this day on, the 90th supplied the hospital located on Long Binh with at least fifty pairs of scissors per week. Once a week, the knives and water pipes were turned over to the MPs for destruction. The amnesty box became a drop-off point for pornographic literature and lewd photographs. You always knew when a large batch had been picked up because the soldiers crowded around the S-3's office.

Gerry White confirmed that there had been no problems among the officers' company except for some general grousing about "more brass bullshit." Bill Huff called and said all had gone similarly well at Camp Alpha. Maybe we had been overly concerned. The processing NCOs at all three points read the President's message to each new group. By the end of the day, some would have it memorized. There was nothing more than some predictable grumbles—especially from the junior enlisted people who thought the NCOs should be tested for alcohol abuse. My report to Lewis assured him that the program was off to a successful start. No one had refused to give a sample.

Then, at about 1500 hours, a fellow lieutenant colonel approached me with tears in his eyes. He confessed that he couldn't pee on command. I found myself following him to a latrine to ensure the validity of his sample, and then presented it to the medics myself.

As it would turn out, this was our biggest problem, and no one had anticipated it. The inability of some soldiers to pee while being watched. A few men had gone through the line two or three times but remained unable to give a specimen. Most officers and NCOs within the 90th were called upon during the next months to help out as I had done for the lieutenant colonel—a solution I am sure would have vexed the staffers at Headquarters. The NCO of the 90th had some difficulty convincing the medics that this was an acceptable procedure, but after a long talk, NCO to NCO, the problem got solved and was never reported up the chain of command.

By late afternoon, the results began to arrive. In the initial group of 180, there were thirty positives. The operations NCO started to process those who tested negative for the next day's flight. The system was working, and it looked as though we would get enough men to fill the next aircraft.

A call from General Martin's office in mid-afternoon informed me that all members of my battalion would have to give a urine sample that same day. By 1700 hours, everyone in the 90th, as well as the MPs and medics at the detox center, had complied. I led the march to the helicopter pad. Of course, the permanent party of the 90th had to endure a good deal of commentary from the transient population. In truth, I was glad they had the opportunity to observe us. It would reinforce the idea that no one was above the rules. But I was secretly concerned about the results. Were there any drug addicts in the battalion? I didn't think so, but I could not be sure.

By the time I had returned to my office, none other than Charlie Connell had stepped off the bus from the Bien Hoa airport. He was full of questions, having overheard the returnees boarding the plane he had just gotten off. I told him we were starting a new football bowl game: the Urine Bowl.

Charlie laughed and said, "Only you could get the assignment of collecting urine samples!"

"Yeah, but remember who's keeping all the statistics."

On the way up to Headquarters, I gave Charlie the same tour Ed had given me three weeks earlier.

Charlie said, "I'm glad to be back." I gave him a funny look.

"Do you remember all those Seiko watches I bought the kids five years ago in Bangkok?" I remembered.

"Well, they're all broken and I have to replace them. Best buy on watches I ever made! What's the price in your PX?"

After dropping Charlie off, I returned to check all the key processing points. The number of soldiers entering the battalion had slowed to a trickle. Therefore, the backup at the front gate had been cleared and the line at the helicopter pad was gone. John Holt confirmed that we had received enough negative test results to fill the next day's flight.

But we were up to about thirty-five positives. The medics said they would have one more batch of returns for us later that night. I asked about the results of the 90th, but they wouldn't be coming until the next day.

General Martin's office had called throughout the day to get the numbers of positives and negatives. They had already named a major to be the command's drug control officer. He was interested in statistics only—not in how the procedures were going.

I had a staff meeting late in the afternoon with the NCOs from the 259th Replacement Company to discuss the day's happenings and receive their recommendations. Having spent much of their time floating among the troops, they reported that most soldiers seemed to take the procedure in stride. A small percentage was hostile, and vocal. But so far, no real resistance had emerged.

In the middle of the meeting, the phone rang. It was a major from USARV Headquarters, the control officer for war trophies.

"Do you still have a 105 Howitzer in the battalion?"

I replied that we did. Today it had flowers decorating its muzzle, put there by some transient, I guess. If I wanted to keep it, said the major, I must fill out form so and so. I said I didn't want it. In that case, he said, I must fill out a different form. I hung up the phone. What a ridiculous job, I thought, keeping track of disabled weapons.

The staff meeting continued. The NCOs recommended that we pull the positives from the formation before announcing the flight manifest. Their logic seemed sound; there would be enough pressure from those cleared to go home to prevent the positives from starting anything that might cause a delay. We all agreed to this procedure, and it remained in place until the end of my tour.

After the meeting I made my rounds. It was just another night at the officers' club. No one seemed concerned about the results of his test. A stop at the steam bath also showed business as usual. Mr. Kim said there had been a lot of discussion about the new procedure, but most comments were about not being needlessly delayed. I stopped by the S-3 shop. We had received the last batch of results from the medics, for a total of thirty-five positives. All were enlisted men, with just a few junior NCOs.

At 2100 hours I arrived at the NCO/EM club for my nightly duty of closing the bar. As usual, my arrival was a signal to the sergeant responsible for running the club to make a last-call announcement—and as usual, it got a round of boos. The band would play one last number. By twenty minutes past the hour, most had departed, but there were always a few who needed a special invitation. This night seemed no different from any other. By 2140 hours everyone was out and the front door locked. The Vietnamese girls who worked there would finish cleaning and wait for the sergeant to escort them to the front gate. There they would go through the employees' shakedown point which was managed by the civilian personnel department and manned by Vietnamese. It was no mystery to me that we never picked up any contraband from them as they left the post. The shakedowns being done by the Vietnamese were a joke

I stopped at the Headquarters building one more time. The S-3 had arranged tomorrow's bus to take the positives to the detox center, and our MPs and security platoon leader were confirmed to wait in the Headquarters building again. I tried Ed, but reached his CQ, who told me that Ed would be at the 90th at 0630 and would have his people in the battalion area. After walking around the area once more, I headed for my trailer to go to bed.

About an hour later, my field phone rang. It was Fred. About thirty-five black soldiers had taken over a barracks in the 259th area. The security platoon leader had his MPs ready to go in and rout them out.

"No!" I said. "I will be right there."

When I reached Headquarters, I saw a cluster of MPs outside the barracks. I ordered them all inside the Headquarters building. Fred said that about an hour ago, the soldiers had descended on the barracks. They forced everyone inside to take their luggage and leave. The people sleeping in the barracks quickly deduced that this wasn't their problem, and had slipped into other buildings to find another place to rest. Fred had spoken to the remaining soldiers through the door. They said they would kill him if he came in. Fred guessed there were more than thirty men holding the building.

After getting as much of the story as I could, I walked across the street and stood in front of the entrance. Fred was standing next to me.

The soldiers called out, "You'll be killed if you come in!" They repeated the same threat to Fred and called him an Uncle Tom. I tried to speak, but was shouted down. It became obvious that no amount of persuasion would do any good tonight. I went back to the Headquarters building and told the security platoon leader to place a guard with a radio at each of the two entrances to the building, and to keep his other people inside Headquarters. I was pretty sure the men in the barracks would not try to leave. They really had no place to go.

I called Ed Murphy. He agreed I should keep my people out of sight and give no show of force. He assured me that he would be down to the 90th tomorrow with his people, but would keep them out of sight.

Next I called Lewis. There was a USARV regulation that any serious incident had to be reported up the chain of command. The regulation included a list of examples a mile long—from fender-benders to murder—and a caveat—when in doubt, report it. Lewis approved of the steps I'd taken and said he would be at the battalion in the morning. I assured him that it wasn't necessary, but he insisted. I didn't want to turn this into a circus. I was sure that when the troopers gave in, they were going to be embarrassed enough without being put on display.

I spent the rest of the night talking with Fred. We went through every possible scenario. All seemed to boil down to the fact that I would have to enter the building, an unappealing challenge.

The night passed quickly. Ed Murphy arrived at 0615 and assured me his people were in place. At 0630 the usual routine for the 259th began. After police call, the troopers reassembled under the shed. The NCO mounted the podium and announced that the first names to be called would have to get their baggage and assemble in front of the bus by the battalion headquarters building—from there, they'd be taken to the detox center. He began to read off the list of thirty-five names that had been caught on yesterday's screening. In all, only eighteen people answered and left the formation. Obviously, some of the remaining seventeen were currently holed up in the barracks.

When I looked in on the proceedings, the positives were

boarding the bus and being checked off the roster. After everyone was on, the MP stepped up in the door well and the bus headed off for the back gate. Indeed, we were short seventeen positives. That meant approximately half of those men in the barracks knew they were scheduled for the detox center.

Colonels Lewis and Gardner arrived. I left them in front of Headquarters to have things explained. My head couldn't take in any conversation with them. I was completely absorbed with the problem of the barracks.

Not really knowing what my next move would be, I walked toward the entrance and yelled, "It's time to come out."

A voice shouted back, "Fuck you, Colonel."

But another voice said, "You can come in to talk, but only if you come in alone." Fred was the only other person in front of the door. He shook his head no.

I opened the screen door and entered slowly. There was no one at my end of the building. The group was clustered in the dark at the far end. I walked about halfway to them, and the spokesman stepped forward. He was a short, thin PFC. He reminded me of Sammy Davis, Jr. He asked me for the results of the urine test. I told him there were seventeen in the group who had tested positive.

"Who are they?"

I had not brought the list with me, so I couldn't answer him.

He said, "We're all ready to come out, but we don't want you fucking us over."

"If you all come out, I'll call the names of those who were positive, and then those men should get on the bus for the detox center. The rest of you will be processed for the next plane. In fact," I added, "some of you were called for this afternoon's plane, but because you didn't answer up, your seats went to others."

This met with a lot of cursing and accusations.

When things settled down, I told them there was a plane tonight that would be manifested this afternoon, and they could be on it. The PFC wanted my assurance that they could say goodbye to the brothers who would not be going home.

"Deal." I turned and left.

I went to Fred immediately to get the list of positives. Slowly the soldiers began to come out. The processing NCO returned with Fred, and I began to call off the names.

One man heard his name and said, "I never used that shit— much."

When the roll call was done, the little PFC told those who were positive to get their baggage and move to the bus. They did.

I noticed Ed Murphy had brought his MPs into the street and that they were all around the bus. The group began to dap and say their goodbyes with complex handshakes. Then as the men moved in clusters toward the bus, things began to come apart. Murphy's men grabbed the first two or three and put them into a spread position against the bus. I caught the movement out of the

Chapter 4 – Gold Flow Begins

corner of my eye. Realizing we were moments away from a fight, I ran toward the bus shouting and waving the MPs away. Ed saw the situation and called out to stop.

The MPs stepped back and the moment passed. It took about fifteen more minutes, and after the bus had pulled away, the PFC who helped defuse the situation disappeared and blended into the group of transients.

My next move was to catch Ed as he was getting into his jeep and ask what the hell his guys were trying to prove. He said there had been a misunderstanding with the NCO, who thought Ed wanted everyone checked for weapons. Red-faced, he apologized and drove off.

I looked up and down the street. All seemed back to normal. I thought about Sandy's comment: *At times you will wonder who helped you through those decisions.* I realized that he'd been correct.

I had forgotten about Gardner and Lewis. When I entered my office, there they were. They had seen the troops boarding the bus and felt optimistic about the future. They said the new policy had been announced countrywide this morning, and that now the troops "knew what to expect." I was not so confident.

As the two were leaving, Gardner handed me a note from General McDowell, which had passed through the chief of staff and through General Martin. It was the results of the investigation of beer found in the 90th Replacement Battalion's steam bath. In his own hand, General McDowell had written, "Tell Campbell he will have to find a better story than that." Gardner looked at me, shrugged his shoulders, and left with Lewis in tow.

I called Major Leavit. "Did you get the report back?" He hadn't. I told him about the note and asked, "What's your next move?"

"I'll have to wait until I receive the report back from the general," he said.

Later that afternoon, I received a call from General Martin. Newspaper reporters and TV film crews would be down tomorrow morning to talk with me and look around. After touring the 90th, they wanted to be shown the detoxification center and urinalysis machine. I was to tell them about the procedures within the battalion.

"We're ready to start," Martin said. "Colonel Brown, the USARV public relations officer, will accompany the group through the tour. If you feel uncomfortable about answering any questions, you should defer to Colonel Brown."

After I hung up the phone, I began to feel uneasy about facing the media. At least there was some good news, though. Following Martin's call, Bill Huff reported that he had three positives out of the day's 200 tests. That made thirty-eight positives out of roughly 700 tested—or about 5.5 percent of the troopers. Not too bad, if the percentage held.

I wasn't looking forward to meeting with the press, especially because there was an evasion for them to sniff out. The only reason for the early start had been to protect the chief medical officer, who had slipped up in his announcement. The new latrine was barely started and the shakedown point at the front gate was less than half completed. The detox was operating—but amid carpenters, plumbers and electricians.

Not having been exposed to the press before, I didn't know exactly what to expect. But I had watched the nightly news for the past five years while I was in the United States. The news about Vietnam had evolved from a very positive perspective in 1966 to a very negative one in 1971. The 180-degree turn seemed to come about as the American public's attitude changed toward the war. Or had the reporting changed the public's view? The press seemed to feel it was their God-given right to expose every detail of the war. I recall one newscast I had watched. An American Marine company had just attacked a VC position and been driven back, having taken a number of losses. In the middle of the chaos, a reporter was pushing his way toward the captain in charge for an interview. The captain was trying to extricate the dead and wounded safely by helicopter, get a resupply of ammo, and begin another attack. As I watched the reporter push his way toward the embattled officer, I was overcome with rage.

The reporter asked the captain, "What are you going to do now?" Had I been that man, I would have said, "Give me that microphone. I want to put it where the sun never shines." I only hoped that tomorrow wouldn't give me the opportunity to use that line. I wanted to keep my career in the Army.

Colonel Brown called from Headquarters to tell me he would arrive at 0900 hours tomorrow with about fifty reporters and a host of TV crews. He assured me that he would be there to help me the whole time. He also said he would bring Captain Hardee along to control the TV crews. They had been asked to film in good taste, and Hardee would help ensure that they did. Fred and I spent most of the evening outlining key points to cover with the press. By the end of the evening, I had many pages of notes. I reduced the pages to key phrases and finally condensed everything to a single 5-by-7-inch card. The rest of the evening and into the night, I kept reviewing my pages of notes, determined not to give the reporters a single thing to misconstrue. I wanted the news people to understand that the army was attempting to save the GIs from this sickness.

CHAPTER 5
VISITORS

My first visit of the day was to the S-3 office to find out how the members of the battalion had done on their test. The operations sergeant was sitting behind his desk, and as I entered, he beamed.

"Good news?"

"Not a single positive result."

I hoped that would be noted at General McDowell's staff meeting this morning.

Early in my tenure as a commander I had come to the conclusion that many of my younger enlisted men, and possibly some of my junior officers, smoked pot. It was a court-martial offense. Proof, however, was so difficult to find that most cases tried at this time were thrown out of court for lack of evidence. You could shake down a man's living area and find pot. But if he denied that the stuff was his, or claimed that someone else had put it there, the burden of proof became the accuser's.

Because of this, I let it be known through the NCOs that I was no longer going to try to catch pot smokers. However, anyone who failed in his duties would be transferred out of the battalion before sunset the same day. And he would go to the unit farthest upcountry on the Demilitarized Zone. The soldiers knew that the transfer could be implemented with relative ease. For six months, the battalion's clean record held. The 90th was the last battalion to lose its perfect record. The first and only person to come up as positive was a cook in the officers' company mess hall. After his return from the detox center, he was immediately transferred upcountry. We never had another positive.

The press arrived on schedule. Colonel Brown and Captain Hardee accompanied a caravan composed of a bus and other assorted vehicles. After the vehicles were off the road and unloaded, Colonel Brown ushered the newspaper reporters into my office. Captain Hardee stayed outside with the TV crews.

We'd placed chairs in my office, but there were too many reporters. Many took up positions around the room, leaning against the wall. There were representatives from all over, including the *New York Times*, the *London Times*, *Time Magazine*, and *Newsweek*.

Colonel Brown introduced me. Unexpectedly, I felt a little flattered at being the center of attention. But I was also very apprehensive. I was a reader of Westerns and decided to follow the gunslinger's advice: always keep your back to the wall. Or in this case, at the far end of the long table and against the window. The light shining in the window would also shroud my facial expressions. At least in this position the questioners wouldn't turn me into a whirling dervish. Colonel Brown finished his introduction and sat at the other end of the table.

After a few words of welcome, I launched into my prepared remarks. I reviewed all our procedures and spoke for five to ten minutes. The first question came from the reporter seated directly in front of me.

"Did you have any resistance? Did anyone refuse to give a sample?"

"No one," I answered.

"What was the reaction on the first day?"

"I would classify their reaction as one of surprise."

Another reporter asked, "What questions were you asked that first morning?"

I repeated for him those that I remembered.

A man in the back raised his hand. "Has anyone that tested positive been shipped out to States before being detoxified?" I repeated our procedure for separating the positives from the negatives and of listing positives off the Univac 1005. As we called the names out, we would do a second check as they boarded the bus. The second check was done by a different person.

"How did you ensure accuracy?"

"Only negative results are posted on the IBM cards that are used to manifest the plane," I answered. "If a positive card is accidently included, it is printed on the manifest sheet. This sheet undergoes many checks prior to loading the bus for the airport."

He was about to pursue the question, but another man asked the other side of the question, "How can you ensure that a person who is negative doesn't accidently get sent to detox?"

"The negative slips are returned separately from the positive ones and are checked by the processing NCO and the people who run the Univac 1005. It is possible for IBM cards to get crossed, but we have two or three reviews on both the positive and negative returns."

Another question came from someone standing against the wall. "Are the medics capable of keeping pace or are we sending planes home with empty seats?"

I assured him things were moving efficiently.

It dawned on me that the questions were the same ones asked in planning the operation. It made me feel good that the four battalion commanders had asked one another the same questions—and that I could respond smoothly now.

The next question was the most obvious one: "How many positives have you uncovered in the first two days?"

I answered with the percentage that was on my report— approximately six percent. The reporter wanted to know the actual numbers. I said there were roughly 35. Was 35 the correct number?

"To be 100% accurate, the number is 38", I retorted. He wanted to know the breakdown by grade.

"I don't know that information."

"Why not?"

Colonel Brown interjected, "It is not his responsibility, and the numbers are available at Headquarters." I thought, *Thank you, Colonel Brown*.

The next questioner asked whether any officers had been positive.

"None have," I said.

There were two questions I was dreading—why we had started a day before the other replacement battalion, and any question involving the soldiers who took over the barracks. I had skipped any reference to the barracks problem in answering the first question I'd been asked. A reporter asked how many I thought would be needing detoxification after a month of operations. I said I couldn't begin to guess.

A question from the front: "Why did you start a day before the other replacement battalion?" Bingo, the sixty-four-dollar question.

I answered, "Because we were ready."

"If you are ready, why isn't the new latrine completed?"

"We knew we wouldn't have it done for another week. The helicopter pad is just an interim solution—especially since we are not yet in the rainy season."

"Why wasn't the 22nd Replacement Battalion ready?"

Colonel Brown again interrupted, saying that he thought it had to do with the delivery of the FRAT machine used to test the urine samples. The reporter remarked that it seemed strange that the program was not implemented at the same time. I let the remark go unanswered.

After the barrage of questions, the group was ready to tour. They gathered outside the Headquarters building and the TV crews got out of their vehicles. Captain Hardee took them down to the 259th processing point and assembled them directly behind the processing NCO, who had been warned about the visit and was looking sharper than usual. He had a group of about twenty returnees whom he had been holding up for the newspaper people.

He began his briefing by reading the President's message, something we had stopped doing the day before because it was now common knowledge among the troops. But he was following the script we had decided on.

While the sergeant was closing his briefing, the TV crews were filming. They took shots of the sergeant, the men, and all the buildings in the area. They even snapped the new latrine going up. The newspaper people began to ask questions of the GIs who were walking back to the helicopter pad to give their sample. Questions ranged from, "Do you use drugs?" to "What do you think of the President's program?" Needless to say, the answers to the first question were uniformly negative. As a matter of fact, there didn't seem to be any obvious users in the group—no one, at any rate, who looked too bad off. But you never knew.

To the other question the answers ranged from, "The Army is fucking me over again," to, "It's a good idea."

The newspaper man who received the latter answer asked, "Do many people use drugs?"

"Sure, some guys are on drugs."

"How many?"

"Who the fuck knows?"

We all went up to the helicopter pad. Again the TV cameras were rolling, and photographers were clicking away for all they were worth. Although the crews never took a direct shot of the men peeing, I wouldn't have been surprised. Captain Hardee was hard-pressed to keep an eye on all of them.

But not too many people wanted to argue with Captain Hardee. He stood about 6'5" and was solid; an imposing exterior that concealed a mild manner that was not on display today. I enjoyed working with the man. He was not assigned to our unit, but would show up with every visiting newspaper or TV crew, which amounted to about four times a week. He and the adjutant who conducted most of the tours became fast friends, and to me, he became like family.

Once the tour concluded, the media walked back to the bus and other vehicles and began to board. The man from *Time* said that this would be the lead article in next week's magazine and that the pictures he took would, in all probability, be on the front page. That night, in writing my wife, I told her to keep her eye out for the story. Weeks went by. Finally, one day, out of her letter dropped an article. It was a short piece from *Time*. What had happened? I discovered later a much bigger story had pushed our story to the back—the Pentagon Papers.

That first day after the journalists departed, I turned to go to the mess hall just as a jeep drove up with General McDowell at the wheel. I invited him in for a cup of coffee, but he was not interested. He wanted to look over the troops.

We walked up the main street. Every time he would see a soldier with an unauthorized hat he would announce, "Get that man in proper uniform!" Headgear in the Army was various and inspired, but the only sort authorized in a garrison was the baseball cap or the green beret. However, almost every unit in Vietnam had its own special headgear. The berets came in every color of the rainbow. Many returning from a line unit had never worn a baseball cap: most had some sort of jungle hat. The 1st of the 9th Cavalry unit wore brown cowboy hats. I pointed out to the general that many of these men didn't own baseball caps, and that in most cases, they wouldn't be in the battalion for more than two days before departing in khaki uniforms—which required garrison hats. No matter, though. General McDowell wanted them in proper headdress. He also pointed out a few whose fatigues were filthy. Most of these were from combat units and the dirt had been ground into the cloth. But it seemed hopeless to point this out. Instead, I tried distracting him.

"Do you want to see the process for obtaining urine samples?" He gave me a hard look. Not interested. We went on our way.

Finally, I gave up, reduced to saying, "Yes, sir. Yes, sir." I decided it was General McDowell's entertainment, pointing out uniform violations. As we approached his jeep, he turned to me and said, "Heard about your battalion's urine test results. Pretty good. Keep up the good work."

He climbed into the jeep and pulled away. So, someone had spoken up at the staff meeting. It felt good to get a compliment.

And from that day on, we kept all the baseball caps discarded by the soldiers after they changed into their khaki uniforms. The NCOs of the 259th gave each incoming man two choices: accept a secondhand hat or go to the PX and buy a new one. Most accepted the secondhand one.

The engineers were putting the finishing touches on the new latrine. Jake Largent stopped by during the afternoon and said we could begin to use it the next morning. I called in Captain Wills and told him to get ready to close down the helicopter pad the next morning.

As he turned to go, he asked, "What will we name the new site?"

Before I could think, I said, *"Pee House of the August Moon."* To this day I still don't know where the inspiration came from. By sundown a sign was over the doorway leading into the latrine. One of the carpenters did a magnificent job of scripting the name in green against a pale blue background.

The next day, Dr. Jaffe, the head administrator of the President's drug program, arrived from Washington, DC for a firsthand look. He was accompanied by a large entourage: General Martin and his drug control staff (which now numbered three officers), the chief medical officer and his staff, plus four or five other civilians from Washington. Dr. Jaffe had already visited the laboratory where the FRAT machine was housed. He was to get a full briefing and tour at the 90th and then go on to inspect the detox center. I remembered a quote by President Nixon in the *Time* article reference to this morning's visitor: "Dr. Jaffe is controversial, he's blunt, he is abrasive."

The group was more than an hour late arriving. When General Martin introduced me, I could see that the administrator was experiencing some discomfort. He was perspiring profusely—normal for a new arrival—but he was also pasty white. As we walked into the Headquarters building to my office one of his staff let me know that he had Ho Chi Minh's revenge, a good case of diarrhea.

I gave my usual briefing. Dr. Jaffe asked some of the same questions as the newspaper people had a few days before. The medical officer rolled out the plans for the detox center on the large table. In the middle of the explanation of the security setup and arrangement of the buildings, the administrator asked in a rather loud voice, "Where is the bathroom?" I told him there was none in the building nor nearby. His face took on a look of panic.

But I hastily added, "My trailer is just down the street."

He said, "Let's go." The two of us walked, then jogged to the trailer. I waited for him on one of the picnic tables. When he came out, he was all over me for the lack of latrine facilities in the battalion. I said we had enough, but that they were located on the perimeter because we had to burn the stuff each day.

"Burn it?"

"Yes, I have twenty Vietnamese come in six days a week to burn excrement." All units did about the same thing. I told him to notice the black smoke as he drove around. It certainly wasn't barbecue smoke. He looked at me with a strange expression, devoid of humor.

We arrived back at the office, where the group was patiently awaiting our return. The medical officer finished reviewing the plans of the detox center. Then we all went out to the processing point. The NCO had a group ready for briefing. The group listened to the entire presentation and then departed for the pee house along with the men.

The total group was so large that not everyone could enter the building. So, Dr. Jaffe, General Martin, and the medical officer went in to observe. From the pee house we moved on to the detox center. This part of the tour was security-focused because Dr. Jaffe was interested mostly in drug trafficking: "What's being done to ensure that no drugs are entering the compound?" We explained that no unauthorized people were allowed in and that both the MPs and the medical staff were given urinalysis. There were no positives, nor were there any at the 90th. The chief medical officer gave an order that these tests be given frequently. General Martin assured him that everyone would be tested both randomly and frequently.

With the medical people, Dr. Jaffe discussed withdrawal pains. The staff pointed out that some people seemed to suffer more than others. Some even had to be restrained.

Dr. Jaffe asked, "When a man is released, how is he processed to the States?"

"He's returned to the 90th and booked on the next available plane."

"Doesn't that expose him to drugs again?"

"No, the battalion area is as clean as we can make it." I explained the shakedown point.

"Are you finding any drugs during your shakedown?" he asked.

"No, not even in the amnesty box. The word is out that you had better rid yourself of drugs prior to arriving."

"What about the Vietnamese who work in the compound?"

"Their people are checked going in and out of the compound," I told him. The answer didn't satisfy him.

"I think drugs are probably available," he argued.

"That could be," I said, "but we are not finding the empty vials on the ground as we did prior to the beginning of the program and shakedown.

The group left the detox center to fly up to Cam Rhan Bay for a visit to the 22nd Replacement Battalion and the other detox center. I was left standing at the front gate of the detox center. John O'Day offered me a ride back to the battalion but I said I would rather walk. My back gate was only about 400 yards down the road.

As I began to say goodbye, General Martin waved me over and into his vehicle. I was surprised, but got into the back seat. He was one of the brightest men I have ever met and I had a great deal of respect for him.

"It's been a tough morning," he sighed.

Most of the problems seemed to stem from the testy attitude of the man from Washington. It was my first exposure to the general when he just wanted a friendly ear.

When I arrived at Headquarters, Fred was there.

"We're going to get a combat engineer company in the battalion to take a urine test."

"Why?" I asked.

"General McDowell visited the unit yesterday. When he got back to USARV, he ordered the test, and the group is due to arrive this afternoon." I didn't care for this. If General McDowell wanted the engineers tested, they must be a sorry crew.

They turned out to be worse than sorry. At first, most refused to get off the truck. Then they sat down in the middle of the street and refused to obey their officers. When I was told this, I called the battalion commander and told him to get his ass down here. I went out to the street and talked with the company commander. We started to walk among the troops. I ordered the men up, and some began to move toward the pee house, but there was a group of about twenty who would not budge. I was worried that others would see them, and that the idea of a successful resistance would spread. If word got out, we could have trouble from now on.

As the men who'd consented finished up and came out, I had them sent back out of the battalion immediately. A few of the seated soldiers began to relent and move to the pee house, but about ten remained on the ground. The company commander was having no success moving them. At about that time, the battalion commander showed up. He was a rough character, and after about thirty seconds of his abuse, the seated troopers began slowly to get up. He personally led them to the latrine, followed them in, and observed them. After they finished, he loaded them on the last truck and told the company commander to get them back to the unit.

He turned to me and apologized.

I asked him, "How can you accomplish your mission with guys like that in the unit?"

He answered, "With difficulty." He jumped into his jeep and took off.

Over the next few months, the program's popularity increased. The first visitors were general officers from USARV and MACV, including the MACV deputy commander, who later became Chief of Staff of the U.S. Army. On some days, three separate groups would pay us a visit. Many COs visited the battalion, and just as we were beginning to run out of generals, their place was taken by congressmen and senators. At times, two or three congressmen would show up together. Many others came alone.

One visitor was Senator Bob Dole. On the day of his visit to the 90th, there was no evidence of his usual wit. I can't blame him. He was experiencing pain in his arm and was also suffering from Ho's revenge. It was a rerun of Dr. Jaffe's visit, including the same hurried, mid-meeting walk to my trailer. He was short-tempered, but most of his wrath was directed against his own staff.

During another visit by Congressmen Dan Rostenkowski from Chicago, General McDowell dropped by—a surprise, since McDowell had never accompanied any of the others. The congressman was a good old boy, obviously streetwise. He listened to the briefing and took the tour, but when it was over he said he wanted to walk around the battalion and talk to some of the soldiers. I looked at General McDowell, who nodded. This was the first time any of the visitors had ever wanted to meet the men. I stepped aside, thinking that the general would want to walk next to him, but another nod indicated I should accompany him.

Congressman Rostenkowski and I began to walk up the street, and the general and his aide fell into step behind. The Congressmen spotted two black troopers sitting on the fifty-five-gallon drums around one of the 259th's buildings. As we approached, I noticed neither soldier had a hat on. As this imposing delegation drew closer, the troopers remained seated. I could feel General McDowell's eyes burning holes in my back.

When we had come right up to them, I introduced them to the Congressman. The conversation went something like this:

"Have you men gotten your results back yet?"

"You're fucking right we did."

"How did you do?"

"We're going home on the next fucking bird."

"What kept you men from using drugs?"

"Man, that fucking stuff will fuck up your fucking system and blow your fucking mind. We never put any fucking foreign substance in our fucking bodies."

The Congressman never batted an eye.

"Congratulations and good luck," he said.

"We'll be out of the fucking army in two days, and then we'll be fucking happy."

All during our conversation they had never moved off the barrels. As we turned to go, I stole a look at the general. He wouldn't even meet my eye.

The visits were so numerous that they became a part of the routine and no cause for excitement. But all during July and August we were visited almost daily by celebrities, newspaper journalists, and TV crews. To us, it seemed as if the actual shooting war had taken a back seat to the Army's war against drugs.

Colonel Gardner, USARV AG, departed for the States and left his job to Colonel Wagner, whom I had never met. He turned out to be a fine soldier, a fatherly man who had been in the service over thirty years. When he visited the battalion, he was not only given the urinalysis tour, but also the grand tour of the battalion. He stayed for lunch, which CWO Campbell ensured was outstanding. Colonel Wagner seemed truly interested in the battalion.

"Do you need any help?" he asked. At that time I was an officer short in the 178th at Alpha.

"I need a captain with some experience," I answered. About a week later, a new captain was assigned to Camp Alpha.

The next step in Operation Gold Flow was to extend the program to newly arriving personnel coming to Vietnam from the States, to test whether troopers were already drug users when they arrived or became addicted in Vietnam. It seemed obvious to the people out in the units that the latter case was true, but Washington wanted hard evidence.

This new requirement didn't place much strain on us. The strength in Vietnam was dropping. The number of replacements had fallen dramatically from its high-water mark of 544,000. New arrivals were also easier to process. Each planeload could be taken through the battalion as a controlled group, as opposed to the more random process of tracking home-bound soldiers who showed up whenever they chose to arrive. The only problem with the new rule was that of scheduling people through the pee house. A big flight would take time to process, delaying returnees. And any delay, no matter how brief, was deadly serious.

The processing of both returnees and new arrivals became routine. Any arriving drug users were sent to detox for treatment, and upon their clearance, they were assigned to their units; but the records that accompanied them noted their drug use, and they were tested periodically. After only a few weeks of this new testing, however, we were certain that the disease had its roots in Vietnam. The first 1,785 results returned only a single positive—negligible when compared to the returnees' addiction rate.

At the same time the program for arrivals was put in place, USARV also sent out roving teams of medics who would visit units to take random urine samples. The choices didn't seem so random, however. Their visits were purportedly directed at all units, but line units seemed to come under scrutiny most often. Drug users were sent to detox and later returned to their units. And thanks to these roving tests, the 90th never had a repeat performance of its experience with the combat engineer company.

One morning as I reached my office, Captain Holt, the S-3, was waiting for me. He did not look well. He had the computer-printed manifest and the punch cards under his arm. He said that the plane had taken off at 0400 this morning but only had seven people booked on it.

"Seven? They must be having a very good time riding home right now. What went wrong?" All I could think of was, *here comes McDowell*!

I had about an hour. I hoped I could get the facts straight. The captain said the population this morning was down to under 100. Yesterday had been a slow day. The plane that departed at midnight took all the cleared people, except for the seven remainders, who went on the 0400 flight. He showed me his phone log to the local units. Most units had very few people due to go home. Some of the men who arrived came late in the evening. He had even kept the pee house open until 10 p.m., but of course the results didn't arrive before the plane's 0400 departure.

I looked through the printout. He was right. Only seven people had cleared by manifest time. The other results hadn't gotten back to the battalion until 0600. No opportunity to get anyone else aboard.

"We're lucky there are no planes scheduled for today and only one for tomorrow".

"Leave the printout and cards on the table," I said. "We'll be explaining this to everyone from Headquarters all day long." I could picture General McDowell at his staff meeting. I could also picture Generals Kelley and Martin blanching at his comments. With this, on top of the performance of the two troopers on the barrels, I imagined that by sunset I would have a desk as my new command.

The call from the front gate came about an hour later. General McDowell had just entered alone in his own jeep. I moved to a chair at the table and quickly reviewed the material once again. I could see the jeep out the window. I now heard the call to attention given by the sergeant major in the outer office. Then McDowell filled the doorway.

"What in Christ's name did you do last night?"

I started to explain. He interrupted. "Do you know how much those seats cost the taxpayer?"

"Yes, sir."

"How much?"

"$200."

"That's right. Why then did you send an empty plane out of

here?" He listened to my explanation, stood up, and waved his hand at me.

"Don't do that again," he said and turned and left.

The phone rang forever. Generals Martin, Wagner, Kelley and Lewis. Over and over again I offered the same story. Martin and Kelley decided to send Lewis and another colonel from DCSLOG to check my records. They arrived at 1000. The papers were still on my table. General Lewis was white-faced with rage, while the other colonel from DCSLOG thought it was funny. I didn't. My ass was still hanging out. The colonel from DCSLOG finally pulled himself together and reviewed the printout. He came quickly to the conclusion that things were beyond my control—I had done everything by the book. General Lewis, on the other hand, wondered if any punch cards had been lost and insisted on visiting the Univac 1005 shop. Of course, no other cards were there. Finally, the colonel told Lewis to give up—I was clean.

"They have to go face the music," he said.

All day the phone rang with advice: "Don't let it happen again." I finally became angry and began to answer back. After Lewis's third call, I got testy.

"Get other people in here. I'll ship them!"

The last Congressmen to visit the battalion that summer was from someplace in Southern California. He arrived alone in the back of a sedan driven by a PFC from Headquarters. From the moment he stepped out, I was impressed. A man in his sixties, he had not one drop of perspiration on his forehead. He wore an immaculate white shirt and a pair of wrinkle-free gray slacks. He wore a panama hat and was smoking a big cigar. He was the coolest looking person I had ever seen in this climate. I gave him the briefing and the tour. He was very soft-spoken, and at times it was difficult to pick up his questions. But when he was asked to repeat them, he did so without anger or annoyance—typical reactions of the powerful.

At the end of his visit, he turned to me and put his hands on my shoulders and said, "Keep up the good work." It was not a politically motivated move—he was serious.

CHAPTER 6
EFFECTS OF THE DRUG PROGRAM

During my tours of the battalion area, I began to notice fewer and fewer drug vials lying around. In fact, it was now rare to find even a single one. I attributed this phenomenon to our thoroughness at the shakedown point plus the program's publicity. By now, everyone knew about it. The amnesty box was popular, too, especially for surgical scissors—the hospital at Long Binh was grateful. They got so many from us that they stopped requisitioning them.

But a new item was being picked up at the shakedown: urine. It was said that clear urine was being sold on the black market at $25 per ounce. Nobody had yet refused to give a sample. They simply tried one ploy or another to circumvent the system, and their ingenuity in slipping it by the MPs was remarkable. Two favorite hiding places were Vitalis hair tonic containers and 35mm film containers. One approach so impressed the MP at the shakedown point that he let the man go, but notified the medical NCO at the urine collection point. The soldier had placed a plastic pouch under his arm. It was taped inside his armpit. The pouch was connected to his penis by plastic tubing that was taped to the inside of his leg and traveled up his side. By the time the man arrived at the pee house, word had spread, and a lot of people had drifted over. When the soldier's turn came, the latrine windows were filled with faces. The medical NCO allowed him to go ahead.

But the contraption wouldn't function. When he admitted defeat, he received an ovation. Soon, the MPs were picking up more urine than any other type of contraband.

The number of women processed through the battalion was small, most through Camp Alpha. But two or three a week were coming through the 381st. Most were nurses. This initially posed a problem: Who would watch them give samples? The solution from Headquarters was that all women could produce their sample without being observed. During the entire time I commanded the battalion, not a single woman tested positive. Depending on one's view of human nature, one might draw different inferences from the facts, but I like to think the women were less susceptible than their male counterparts.

Some of the women passing through were very helpful. I had been getting complaints that waitresses in the NCO/EM club were short-changing customers, so on one occasion, I asked two nurses to help search the packages and clothing of the Vietnamese women leaving the compound. The Vietnamese were not allowed to have American scrip in their possession (i.e., temporary currency issued by the American military in lieu of dollars, which were not legal).

One night after closing, the nurses posted themselves in the civilian shakedown point which was ordinarily manned by two Vietnamese, one male and one female. The NCO who ran the club arrived with about twenty waitresses leaving work. The first walked up to the shed, and within seconds we could hear a long string of impassioned Vietnamese issuing from inside. The other girls immediately sat on the ground in the darkest area they could find. After the first of the women left the shed, the rest went through one by one. As it turned out, the nurse had picked up scrip from the first girl, but found no contraband on anyone else. A search of the area where the girls had been sitting yielded almost $100 in scrip and three small bottles of liquor. The first girl was fired, and I hoped the nineteen others would take heed. I repeated this approach two more times during the next few months and got similar results.

Later during a visit to the officers' club on Long Binh, I noticed that the bartender was the woman who had been caught. She gave me a big smile. My call the next day to the civilians who did the hiring was met with disdain. She was only barred from returning to my NCO/EM club. She could be hired anywhere else in the club system—including my officers' club. I told the civilian at the other end of the phone, "Over my dead body." If she were sent to work here, I would personally escort her back to him.

The next official step in closing the circle around the drug users was to take urine samples from people going on R&R or leave. That meant a bigger work load at Camp Alpha. Bill Huff and I met to discuss the details.

Timing was a problem. Most commands, especially the local units, would have their people report in the morning for an afternoon departure, or else the night before for the 747 leaving each noon for Hawaii. But the medics at Long Binh could only promise a twenty-four-hour turnaround. Bill could not rely on them to meet the shorter departure schedule.

Bill had latrine space and enough medics to man the latrines. A call to General Martin's drug control group revealed that either a machine would have to be installed at Alpha, or the number of R&R days would have to be routinely increased by one. The issue was bandied back and forth for a few days. The lost time was unacceptable to the commanders, but there were no more machines in Vietnam. Finally, it was decided to fly another machine into Alpha from the States.

While the debate was going on, Bill and I tried to guess how many soldiers would test positive. We both felt the number would be small. People who went on leave and R&R had to have money. People on drugs never had money for anything but their habit— even though heroin was cheap. We estimated we'd get less than one percent.

As it turned out, we were high. Even though we hadn't announced the new program to the troops, it was over a week before we picked up our first offender. In February, drug urinalysis for soldiers heading out on R&R and leave was curtailed to a ten-percent sample because positives were so rare.

Charlie Connell was kept busy churning out statistics, compiling percentages on drug use by race, grade, education, and so on. But his figures were closely guarded. They were never published in Vietnam for public consumption. Nevertheless, because of my close friendship with Charlie, I learned that the percentage of black and white users, when adjusted for population size, was equal. Sixty days after the beginning of the program, the majority of users were junior enlisted men. There was a small percentage of NCOs, a few junior officers, and not a single woman. Later studies indicated that the military expected most addicts to be black or Chicanos from disadvantaged backgrounds. Yet, by contrast, more than seventy percent of all military addicts were white. They typically came from small Midwestern or Southern towns, had no history of hard drug use, and lacked obvious character disorders.

But if Charlie and the USARV staff dealt with cold statistics, the people of the 90th dealt with the drug problem in quite a different way. Even though most people in the 90th took verbal— and sometimes physical—abuse from the drug users, it was hard not to feel sorry for them and want to help.

One unkempt young enlisted man who arrived in the battalion to catch his flight home couldn't have weighed more than ninety pounds, and it was obvious his departure would be delayed. The processing NCO talked with him alone and found him to be very intelligent. He claimed he was a college graduate. Nevertheless, he was clearly disoriented. He would immediately forget whatever he'd been told. The NCO found him a few hours later wandering aimlessly. He couldn't remember if he'd given his sample. The NCO took him by the hand to the collection point and guided him through the process. Then he took him to the barber shop to get him shaved and sheared. Next he took him to the mess hall and had the cooks prepare some food, which the boy only picked at. The next morning the same NCO knew he would have to read off the boy's name from the list of positives. But by now he was so taken by the boy's plight that he asked another NCO to take over his duties. Then he helped the boy get his gear together, put it in the jeep, and drove him to the detox center.

This behavior among the processing NCOs was not unusual. I witnessed one of them call a final bus loading list, miss a person, and then hand the list to another NCO so he could go search for the missing man. In fact, one day, the processing NCO threw the list to another NCO and said aloud, "That son of a bitch isn't going to miss this flight!"

He ran up the street toward the back of the compound, obviously heading for the NCO/EM club. A few minutes later he returned with a smaller man in tow, a sergeant who was having difficulty keeping up with the NCO's strides. When he got to the door of the bus, the processing sergeant called out to this buddy, "This is Murphy," and then proceeded to take him up the steps of the bus and seat him. The NCO climbed off the bus, covered with perspiration.

He said, "If Murphy missed this one, I was going to turn in my stripes." It turned out that Murphy had missed two previous flights because of his love of beer.

Another day I was talking with a processing NCO just after the buses pulled away. He was shaking his head, and I asked what was wrong.

"We went one short." He just couldn't find this kid. He had looked everywhere. Just then a young man in khaki approached us and asked if he'd missed the bus. The sergeant looked at him with fire in his eyes.

"Yes, you did, son. However, you are a lucky bastard today. See that bus at the front gate? Well, it's ready to go out the front door. Maybe if you break the record for the 800 meters, you can catch it." The boy sprinted off, and the sergeant chuckled. The bus was picking up the officers and would be stopped there at least another ten minutes.

Another man, obviously detox material, decided one day that noon was a good time to take off all his clothes. He began streaking around the main drag. At first the members of the 90th attempted to catch him, but he was too quick, and their unsuccessful tries brought only laughter and cheers from his fellow transients. Finally they let him go and picked up his clothes to take to the orderly room at the 259th for safekeeping. About four hours later, two other transients brought him in. The guy had the shakes and his eyes were rolling in his head. They dressed him as best they could and took him to the detox center. The sergeant there didn't want to accept him at first, but my men convinced him the paperwork would follow, which it did.

The problem touched us all, at one point or another. One night, I was making my customary late tour. Toward the back end of the compound, across the street from the 18th Company's mess hall, ran a shallow drainage ditch. As I was cutting across the roadway on my way to look in on the snack bar, my eye caught a reflection. At first I thought it was just the water running through the ditch. Everything was extremely dark—as usual, the rainstorm we had had earlier in the evening had blown out a few lights. But something made me go over to look. There lying in the ditch was a trooper. I knelt down. The man's face was half submerged, but the water level was low and his nose was not covered. He was breathing. I tried in vain to lift him and roll him out of the ditch. He wasn't large, but he was absolutely dead weight. I looked around—no one was nearby.

"Help!" I yelled. I was afraid to leave the man alone because he might roll over and drown.

Finally, a head appeared from the door of the barracks just

above me. The man's comment was oddly polite. "Don't you know people are trying to sleep?"

It had to be a new arrival. I cried out, "Mister, get your ass down here right now." He ran down, looked at the man, and took a step backward.

I said, "Give me a hand, grab his legs." He finally caught on, and between the two of us, we rolled the man out. His breathing was somewhat irregular, but he appeared to be uninjured. He didn't seem to have been attacked. When the medic arrived in his jeep, we got the man into the vehicle, returned to the aid station, and put a call in to the doctor. No answer. We put the man back into the jeep and sped to the detox center. The medic at the detox got the duty doctor up, and he took a look at him. His diagnosis was that the soldier was stoned.

As for my battalion surgeon, his absence from the incident was the last straw. He had been in a combat unit for the first nine months of his tour, and was now afraid to come out of his hooch after dark. He was afraid, he said, of being "fragged," something he had seen happen in his old unit. Fragging was becoming popular in the combat units. It was conducted against officers and NCOs. Bombs would be put in places one frequently used – beds, jeeps. The doctor just wanted to hang on until his time in Vietnam was over. He never wore a uniform, just shorts, a green t-shirt, a jungle hat, and combat boots with no socks. And he was incorrigible.

The next day I went up to the USARV and complained bitterly about my battalion surgeon. With the drug program in full swing, I needed a good doctor now. By the end of the week I had a new one, and my present doctor was reassigned to—of all places—the detox center. The new man was named Ed Watt and had just arrived in the country. He was eager, and I liked his attitude. He said he could learn more in a year in Vietnam than in five years in the States. His goal was to be a plastic surgeon, and when he wasn't busy, he was forever pursuing people to remove their warts, growths, and birthmarks.

Some returnees didn't even wait for the drug test results. They simply turned themselves in. The first time this happened, the NCO on duty didn't know what to do. But as it became more common, we worked out a deal with the detox center to bring these people up right away. Most who turned themselves in seemed to be sincere about getting the monkey off their back.

This group didn't comprise a high percentage of our detox patients, however. Most people who were positive claimed they never shot up and that the results must be a mistake. But closer questioning would reveal that, at the least, they smoked marijuana and would put powdered heroin in a slit in the cigarette.

Another frequent complaint was that we let alcohol abusers off scot-free. One night the security platoon leader found a young trooper rolled into a ball in the dark alley behind the PX storage yard. Try as he might, he could not get the boy to relax and stretch out. Ed Watt, whose hooch was just up the street, showed up quickly. To get the boy uncurled, Ed had to give him a shot of muscle relaxant. After a few hours in the aid station, it was obvious he was going through withdrawal, and the doctor took him up to the detox center.

More and more transients were going into withdrawal within the battalion area. In a desperate attempt to get home, many tried going cold turkey just before they came to us and would be hit by the withdrawal pains while waiting to be processed. Each day we would send a few of these to the detox center.

Another problem facing the battalion was the turnover of NCOs. Because of the twelve-month tour of duty in Vietnam, the battalion was constantly losing people. It became hard to fill the vacancies with competent performers. All units within Vietnam had this problem, which further contributed to a breakdown of morale.

Of course we had an advantage over everyone else since we were in the business of processing replacements and had a chance to look them over. We also had a relationship with the assignment staff at USARV. I asked the people in the 18th Replacement Company to keep their eyes open for good NCOs. I also directed the USARV personnel located within the battalion to give me the records of the top three NCO grades who were returning to Vietnam for the second or third time—especially those who had been wounded on previous tours.

When I received such a record, I would search out the NCO and introduce myself. Most weren't happy about being in Vietnam again. If I liked the man, I would take him over to the processing point—the 259th or the 18th—where the next NCO was scheduled to depart to the States. Then I would ask him to watch what the person was doing and leave him. At the next formation I'd seek him out and ask whether he felt he could do the man's job. If the answer was yes, which it usually was because the guy wanted to avoid going back to a combat unit, I would get him assigned to us.

Over a period of months in the summer of 1971, most of the battalion NCOs rotated to the US. All were replaced with people who were in Vietnam for at least their second, but usually their third time. Using my strategy, the battalion built up an NCO cadre that was second to none. Not one NCO selected in this manner turned out to be a disappointment. They were mature people who at first didn't like the drug users they had to deal with, but after a few days of seeing people in trouble, became like sympathetic fathers to these youths. Their assistance and kindness were not always appreciated, but they seldom failed to show compassion. And they had a tough job: they were the bearers of bad tidings. Soldiers full of hatred and frustration with the country, the Army, and the situation lashed out.

John Holt departed, and Major Johnson arrived. Connie Johnson had excellent credentials, and he lived up to them. He was quick to appreciate the problems associated with his job, which had become more complex with the urinalysis program. He also took a great burden off of me. Because of his rank, he could help bear the brunt of officers' complaints, which were the same as those of the enlisted men: "I should have been booked on the plane ahead of this or that person." "I have been here two days and I can't pee." "The food is lousy." "The water in the shower is cold." "The mattress is damp." The last was common during the rainy season. We usually took the time to listen. In most cases we couldn't help, but the complainer always felt better for having vented his feelings to a receptive ear. I often thought, where have these guys been for the last year? But they seemed to look upon the 90th as an extension of home. They had made it this far and expected our accommodations to rival the Holiday Inn.

Rotations continued throughout the summer months. The CO of the 259th was replaced by Captain Jackson, the man who used to count the number of cigarettes in Lewis's ashtray. He was delighted to get away from Headquarters and into the job. The adjutant, Captain Enright, also departed. I selected Captain Black from a pile of records. He was a college graduate, a two-year ROTC man with a degree in English. Again, thanks to Jack Dickey's intercession at Headquarters, Black was assigned to the 90th rather than to a Headquarters staff job. Captain Wills, the S-4, also rotated. He was replaced by Lieutenant Worth. But the biggest problem facing me was the commander at Camp Alpha. The job needed a mature person who was a least a major. He would be dealing with all ranks—including generals—passing through on R&R and leave. He would have the same problems I faced at Long Binh, except for the maintenance of a compound that was constantly falling apart.

During my visits to Headquarters, I was constantly being cornered by Major Jack Charles. who was working in the awards and decorations staff group and hated shuffling paper twelve hours a day. He had heard that the job at Alpha was coming open. At first he merely asked me to consider him for the assignment. But as the weeks went by, his pleas became more dire, and he even took to calling me at the battalion. Meanwhile, I had been reviewing records of new arrivals without much success. Then one day, as Charles was talking to me in the Headquarters hallway, I remembered my own pleas to Colonel Gardner. Right then and there I decided that if Charles wanted the position that much, he would do a good job. It took another week to spring him from his boss. Jack was elated.

One Sunday afternoon I was jogging down the battalion's main street and saw General McDowell. He was headed toward me driving his own jeep again. I stopped and waited, but he drove by without even a nod of recognition. I was angry that he had gotten into the compound again without my knowing it. I had all sorts of early warning procedures set up with the MPs. But of course, they couldn't reach me because I was out jogging.

McDowell drove up the street about a hundred yards beyond me and pulled off the roadway. I turned to jog back up to where he had stopped, but then decided, the hell with it. I watched him walk between the barracks in the 18th Replacement Company area and disappear. He returned in a few minutes, got back in, and drove out the back gate. I wondered if he would notice that the road to the detox center was now named Campbell Drive, thanks to a good-humored new commander of the transportation brigade at Long Binh. After my people noticed the signs, which had been erected in the dead of night as a joke, they had kidded me that roads are normally named after people who are dead.

About a week later, I received a note from McDowell, handwritten on a form used for short memos. It had passed through Chief of Staff General Martin, to AG Colonel Wagner, to Colonel Lewis, to me. Each party had initialed the note and forwarded it along for an answer: "*Last Sunday during a visit to the 90th Replacement Battalion, I came upon a pile of chicken bones outside of Building BX 14-79. Why were they there?*"

My first reaction was to laugh. I called both Connie and Fred in. They thought it funny, also.

I asked Fred, "What kind of a building number could BX 14-79 be?" Neither Fred or Connie could come up with an answer.

"McDowell was in the 18th Company's area on Sunday when he passed me on the roadway," I mused. So we walked up to the company area. There on the corner of each building was a white wooden sign with numbers 102, 103 etc. But next to each sign was another—in faded black letters—part of an old engineer numbering system. The mystery number BX 14-79 was a transient barracks. Returning to the office, I picked up my pen and wrote:

Lewis, Wagner, Martin, Chief of Staff (Info)

To General McDowell:

On Sunday last, we had chicken for lunch. Obviously someone was feeding his dog.

I sent it off hoping this would be the end of things. One fortunate turn was that General McDowell never found out he came to be called "Chicken Bones" by every member of the 90th.

But that week, something larger was afoot. Connie Johnson informed me that a snafu had occurred, and a reporter had gotten wind of it. The wrong man—a sergeant—had been placed in the detox center. He had been held for two days and each of his urine samples had come back negative. Nevertheless, the sample in our records was labelled positive in big red letters. The sergeant had been a general's driver and very active in the support of a Vietnamese orphanage. By the time Connie finished presenting the case, the man sounded positively saintly. General Martin had called and also Lewis, telling us to process him out immediately. Connie said that the first sergeant of the 259th had gone to pick him up and the man was now in the area. He was to be booked on the flight going out this evening.

I walked across the street to check with the people in the 259th about the sergeant's welfare. The commander informed me that he had been very irate. He was going public with the foul-up when he got back to the States. I asked where he was and was told he was sitting outside on one of the fifty-five-gallon drums. Indeed he was, and he refused to budge.

I went out and tried to talk with him. But the conversation was one-sided. He was going directly to the press to tell them what had happened. He would also tell the press about all his good works in Vietnam—which he listed for me. I tried to apologize but he was having none of it. I considered the man's state of mind and I believed he would be true to his word.

It seemed wise to inform Headquarters. So, I called Lewis and warned him of what the sergeant had said. But what I failed to do was to follow up my phone conversation with a written report.

We booked the sergeant on the evening plane and I forgot about him. A week later, I received a call that Colonel Wagner wanted to see me at Headquarters. When I arrived at Wagner's office, there sat Lewis, the deputy AG, the head of the drug control program, and Colonel Brown from public relations. I could tell by their expressions that this was not going to be one of the happier moments of my life. Colonel Brown reported that the sergeant had indeed gone to the press and that the story had hit the papers back home. Others chimed in, everyone talking as if they had not been warned of that possibility a week earlier.

"Did the sergeant say anything about going to the press?"

I looked at Lewis, but he was fumbling for a cigarette and not looking in my direction. I recounted my conversation with the sergeant to the group.

"Did you report this?"

Still, Lewis was not looking my way.

I said, "I believe I reported it to Colonel Lewis's people." I didn't want to make him look bad, but at least I was giving him a chance to go back and pretend to check or to come clean—when in fact I had reported it to him personally.

Lewis said, "None of my people were ever informed."

Nice answer. He didn't exactly lie since he said nothing about himself. Case closed. I received all sorts of admonitions, advice, and the old standard — "Don't let it happen again." I hardly heard any of it. I was mentally calling Lewis every name I could think of. After the meeting, Lewis left with dispatch. I pondered whether to follow him, but I argued myself out of it. If I went, I probably would wind up in more trouble.

The result of all this was that I received a letter of reprimand, the first and only one of my career. It was given to me by Lewis but it was signed by the Adjutant General, Colonel Wagner. He said it would not be forwarded to my files in Washington, DC, but it would be held in my field records and withdrawn when I left Vietnam. No mention of his part, no words of sorrow, no gratitude for not putting him on the spot.

After he gave me the letter, I asked him not to visit the battalion in the future except on business. He looked hurt and asked about attendance at monthly officers' dinners. I told him especially not to come to the dinners because I was withdrawing my invitation as of this very moment. My relationship with Colonel Lewis was restricted after the incident. I gave him credit, though. He never visited the battalion again, either socially or on business.

The number of people being picked up as positive within the battalion remained constant at about 6 to 7 percent. However, the extra people caught by the roving teams sometimes overloaded the detox center's resources. There was another detox center at Cam Rhan Bay, and we had to send people there to cut down on the overcrowding. The MPs would provide guards to prevent them from trying to escape. And when their treatment was complete, these people would not process back through the 90th, but instead go directly from the detox center to an Air Force plane at Bien Hoa.

Generally, as people were detoxified, they would return to the battalion for out-processing on their Freedom Bird. This procedure came to an abrupt halt late one evening. A group was taken to the Bien Hoa airport by a young lieutenant from the 259th. The pilot of the commercial aircraft contracted for the flight questioned the lieutenant as he was unloading the buses outside the terminal, "How many 'heads' [drug addicts] are in the group?" The lieutenant told him there were fifty. The pilot refused to fly them. The lieutenant was in a tough position. He didn't relish giving the news to the men. But he had no choice. The pilot absolutely refused to fly with drug users onboard. As the lieutenant began to call the names of those who would return to the battalion, the troopers began to get uneasy. Nevertheless, he got them aboard the buses and back to the compound.

The next morning, I reported the incident to Lewis by phone. I also had my S-1 write up a report which landed on Lewis's desk that afternoon, carbon-copied to everyone I could think of. This turn of events put the drug control staff personnel into a lather. Their only other option was to start flying these people to the States aboard military medical evacuation planes. Finally, it was decided to treat the drug users as patients—they would return to the US in their pajamas. We would continue our detoxification in Vietnam as before. Those getting out of the service would be out-processed at Oakland or Fort Dix. Those who still had time to serve would be processed to their next duty station with their medical records indicating that they were drug users.

The S-3 came in one afternoon to my office with some dour news. The security platoon leader had just found a man dead in his bunk at the guard barracks.

We both went over. The doctor was already there and confirmed the platoon leader's fears. The initial diagnosis, later confirmed by an autopsy, was that the boy had overdosed on drugs. I couldn't believe it. During our inventory of his possessions, we discovered he was nineteen years old and had just arrived from Hawaii, his previous duty station. He had been here fifteen days. In his personal effects were photos of him tending marijuana plants on the back porch of his Hawaii barracks. His fellow guards said he couldn't wait to get his hands on some of the pure stuff here in Vietnam.

"We warned him of the potency of the Vietnam heroin," they said, "but he wouldn't tell us where he had gotten his drugs."

One of the most difficult things I ever had to do in my career was to write the young man's parents a letter. The circumstances did not suggest that he had died under heroic circumstances. But he did. Like the majority of the other enlisted people, he was young and suddenly found himself in Vietnam defending his country. But he had just come from a society that didn't care about the war and who criticized those who, in their minds, were foolish enough to go fight in it.

What had gone through his mind? What went through the minds of all the other young people in Vietnam? Hard to say. Their first thought was, of course, to stay alive and get back home. They could follow the American public's attitude toward the war through the radio and newspaper coverage. I believe many thought they had been deserted by the people of their country and misdirected by their leaders. Indeed, when the complete history of the war is written, the biggest strategic coup many turn out to be the introduction of drugs to the American forces. The North Vietnamese knew the American people's attitudes and the doubts that ran through the American soldiers' minds. Drugs were an escape—an understandable need—and it eroded discipline and broke morale. This lad was a Vietnam war casualty—as much as if he had been killed in battle by an enemy bullet. We conducted a formal military ceremony to pay him homage.

As Doctor Watt and I sat eating dinner at the 90th officers' club, the loudspeaker system cut away from the music: we were both to report to Headquarters. As we drove down the street in my jeep, I thought someone must be hurt badly if they wanted the doc. He knew it too, and neither of us said a word. As we pulled up in front of Headquarters, the duty officer greeted us. He said the doc had some patients awaiting him at the aid station. Ed jumped into the driver's seat and took off. Someone had gone crazy in one of the barracks. He had taken a bunk adapter and struck about ten sleeping men in the head. As far as the captain could tell, all the wounded were in serious condition.

The captain had called in our MP roving patrol to find the attacker, but to no avail. He had melted back into the population. I went with the captain to the barracks. As I walked through, there was no sound or movement except snoring and the rustle of sleeping men. I went outside and a young enlisted man stepped out of the shadows. At first, I thought he might be the attacker. After the initial surge of fear, though, I could see that he wasn't— but he said he could identify the assailant.

We went back to Headquarters. The witness was pale.

"I saw everything. I'm glad I was lucky enough to escape."

"Fred, put him up somewhere for the night," I ordered. We decided that at 0430 the next morning we would muster all the transients. This was a procedure we used periodically to catch malingerers. It never failed to net one or two who had been hiding, hoping to avoid reporting to their new units.

I stopped by the aid station to see how Ed Watt was doing

with his patients. When I opened the door, I was shocked at the amount of blood covering the outer room. Six people were lying on the floor with bandages wrapped around their heads. In the back room Ed was pressing a bandage down on the head of a man sitting on the operating table. Ed saw me as I entered the room and inadvertently took his hand away from the man's head. Blood from the wound shot up in the air and covered both Ed and the patient. He immediately clamped the dressing back down. I was afraid everyone would have to be evacuated to the post hospital.

"No, nothing that serious," Ed said. "Only superficial head wounds. I'll have them ready to go to the States in the morning."

Next morning, the red star cluster burst in the sky—the signal to the members of the 90th to begin to assemble all the transients on the large field. As usual, there was a lot of bitching and moaning. After each company commander reported that every building had been cleared, we began to call off the names. As each man's name was read, he would pass by an NCO to show his ID card. The young trooper who said he could recognize the culprit was standing next to me. About seventy-five percent of the names had been called out, and I began to think we were not going to catch our man. But at last the young man pulled at my sleeve and said, "Here he comes."

He was a big black man, a PFC from a combat unit, if the patch on his uniform shirt was correct. I stopped him and told him to come with me. He didn't resist but mumbled something about fucking the Army.

As I questioned him in my office, he denied that he was the culprit. But when I produced the witness, he confessed.

"Why?" I asked. He replied, "I don't know—I felt like it."

I knew that by the afternoon, I would have no case against him. Both the witnesses and the injured soldiers would be on a plane bound for the United States. All were people due out of the Army in a matter of days.

I asked him if he would accept Article 15 as punishment. He smiled, knowing I had limited punishments under that portion of military justice. In about three minutes the trial was over and the sentence given. I reduced him to PVT E-1, the lowest grade in the service, and fined him $50.00. He smiled, believing he had beaten the rap. Knowing his urine sample was positive, I had the Sergeant Major take him directly to the detox center. The witness and the injured soldiers departed that afternoon, looking more like Arab sheiks than soldiers. Most of them, had they stayed with their units, would have ridden the sick book for as long as possible. But the lure of going home made them push aside the pain—nothing was going to stop them from getting on that plane.

The trooper who identified the culprit was a brave man. I don't feel that he agreed with the punishment I meted out, but neither he nor the accused realized that a PVT E-1 is not entitled to any veteran's benefits.

That afternoon, I received a note from General McDowell responding to my reply to the chicken bones memorandum. It had traveled the same route as his previous correspondence. It said, "You *have too many dogs down there. Clean them out.*" "Clean them out?" I asked aloud. "How the hell do I do that?"

CHAPTER 7
BEGINNING OF THE END

During the fall of 1971 it became obvious that America's strength in Vietnam was falling rapidly. Entire units were departing. The last group to leave the country consisted of the men selected to carry their unit's colors back to the States. More and more of these color guards were being processed through.

The number of replacements dropped off dramatically, as well. Therefore, I decided to close down the mess hall in the 18th Replacement Company. CWO Campbell's estimates showed we could feed both replacements and returnees in the 259th's mess, and it was also becoming more difficult to replace cooks. I was happy to see the mess closed. It had never been a pleasant place to eat, and besides, CWO Campbell's time was getting short and his position would not be filled when he left. This gave the S-4 one fewer mess to worry about.

The number of people in the mess halls never approached the number of troopers actually housed in the battalion at the same time. Although replacements ate in the mess, the returnees preferred the snack bar, NCO/EM club, or the PX hot dog stand. They were as sick of the mess hall as they were of C rations. Hamburgers and junk food made home seem closer.

A few days before CWO Campbell left, he came to see me.

"I want to have a battalion officers' cookout," he said, "and I'll prepare it all myself."

"That's kind of strange," I said. "We should be treating you." He would have none of it, so I said okay.

The next morning when I left my trailer, the chief was lighting the grill, and next to the barbecue was the biggest steamship round of beef I had ever seen. I made the mistake of asking him where he got it.

He looked at me with disdain. It is an unwritten law in the Army that officers never ask NCOs or warrant officers this question. These groups have their own informal network. If it weren't for these connections, I don't think the Army could operate. That night, approximately thirty people ate the entire steamship round. The bone was so clean not even the stray dogs would give it a second look. Later I found out through another source that the roast had come out the back door of the general officers' mess at Long Binh. If only General McDowell had known!

Connie, Fred, and I met to figure out how we would comply with General McDowell's order to clean out the dog population. McDowell was right. We did have an inordinate number of dogs. They came from the returnees, who would appear at the front gate with their pets. After the owner left, of course, the pet stayed, and GIs can't resist feeding strays. Many people in the 90th kept pets. But these were registered and had had the necessary shots.

Besides dogs, we also had monkeys, cats, snakes, and goats.

But the dog population was out of control. If we scared them off the compound, they would return. We discussed poison, but that could lead to all sorts of complications. The solution we settled on was to shoot them—not a pleasant alternative, but no one had any better ideas.

The following Saturday was designated as "the day." The idea was to collect all the legitimate pets in the staff's trailer compound. The MPs would provide four teams of two men each to patrol with shotguns. Any animal left unclaimed became fair game. Two of the 259th people volunteered for the hunt. Both had been bitten and suffered through an excruciating series of rabies shots.

The following Saturday started off according to plan. But then came the actual shooting. Many rounds were fired. Few dogs were hit. After the first shots, most ducked under the barbed wire and vanished. I called things off—it was a distasteful business, anyway—and wrote a note back up to McDowell indicating compliance with the directive.

The MPs disposed of the dead dogs, but it didn't dawn on me to ask where. A few days later, we had a monsoon storm—typical for that time of year. When the waters subsided, there on the main roadway were the carcasses.

I called Joe Stanley and told him, "Get that same dumb son of a bitch who buried the dogs in the swamp! He's got to remove the remains." The smell was permeating the entire area. Two MPs showed up with a jeep, trailer, and shovels. And they showed true GI ingenuity: they were wearing their gas masks.

Early one morning, Captain Jackson, the CO at 259th, came barging into my office. He was beside himself. The plane due out at 0200 hadn't flown, and the passengers had to be returned. But along with the passengers someone had brought back two stewardesses, and they were presently in a hooch in his area. The line of men outside the hooch was a block long.

Connie Johnson went with Jackson to break up the good time while I departed for a meeting with Lewis. The ladies, it seems, had been afraid to stay on the plane. Some returnees had concealed them on the bus, set them up in the hooch, and let the world know about it. The ladies were obliging. Connie had them transported back to the plane, their overnight bags now bulging with favors received in exchange for services rendered.

My visit with Lewis had been to discuss USARV's ideas concerning Camp Alpha. The Air Force had presented a plan to the MACV headquarters recommending that they take over part of it. The Air Force, which was responsible for the civilian air terminal at Tan Son Nhut, was getting pressure from the Vietnamese to reduce the military presence there. The Air Force wanted the Army to give up the processing building at Alpha. They wanted to cut the area in two and separate the processing building from the rest of the camp by a chain link fence. All departing military personnel, both Air Force and Army, would report to the new Air Force operations building and be bused to the planes. For the last six years, Air Force people and MACV returnees would show up two hours prior to plane time at the civilian air terminal. No one would process through a unit.

The Air Force plan had merit. However, if the processing building were taken away from Alpha, there was no single building properly equipped or large enough to process people on flights for R&R and leave. The Air Force plan would completely destroy the continuity of operation at Camp Alpha. Lewis said that the Air Force was to present its plan to General Mapes, DCSLOG for MACV, next Sunday afternoon and that he and I would be on hand to present the Army side. So we worked up our counterpoints and prepared a staff paper on our position.

The following Sunday I met Lewis at MACV. Headquarters was located in the suburbs of Saigon, near Tan Son Nhut Airport. The building was huge; it was where General Westmoreland and now General Abrams were headquartered. Colonel Lewis had made the trip to Saigon in a sedan, but I traveled down Route 1 in my jeep. I had left early in the morning, taking advantage of the time to also talk over the Alpha operation with the new CO, Major Charles. By now, Jack Charles had settled in and had been told about the Air Force plan. He contributed some good points against it, so I had invited him to the briefing.

Outside General Mapes's office, the Army representatives sat on one side of the waiting room. We had only a few papers. The Air Force sat on the other side. They had reams.

At the appointed time, we were all ushered into the general's office. General Mapes was a crusty old soldier with probably over thirty years in the military. The Air Force brass began their presentation. They talked about the pressure from the Vietnamese and evoked the possibility of terrorist attacks. As an example, they cited the explosion in the terminal five years earlier. Since I had been a victim of this attack, I felt a twinge, realizing I would be arguing against a plan that would prevent such a thing from happening to others.

General Mapes listened as the Air Force leaders stepped through their plan. They had engineering drawings that showed how Alpha would look after they occupied the processing building.

After they finished, General Mapes looked at me.

"What do you have to say?" That his comment was directed at me rather than at Colonel Lewis surprised me. I looked at Lewis and he gave me the okay to go ahead.

I asked the general, "Have you ever seen Camp Alpha, sir?"

"Yes."

"Can you appreciate how efficiently we operate?"

He didn't reply. So I stood and leaned over the drawing now spread out before him. I pointed out how the loss of the building would hamstring our operation and that the added congestion— of people and vehicles—could increase the possibility of a terrorist attack. I pointed out that at some time, as the American strength abated, the Army might need to close the battalion area at Long Binh and do all the processing at Alpha. Without the processing building, the Army would be unable to do so.

The rest of the meeting consisted of arguments presented and rebutted by the two sides. When General Mapes had heard enough, he dismissed us. He would tell us his decision before the week was out. Outside in the hallway Lewis, Charles and I were asking each other how we'd done. We decided we had a 50/50 chance of victory.

Lewis departed for Long Binh. I drove Major Charles back to Alpha and then left for the battalion. The Sunday traffic on Route 1 was, as usual, unbearable. Every person who owned a Honda scooter was out for a Sunday ride. Some Hondas carried entire families; husband driving, one child between his legs, and wife and baby on the rear fender. I often marveled at the cooperative balancing act that took place on those vehicles. Halfway home, I spotted a sedan off on the shoulder. The hood was up and two people were staring into the engine compartment. It was Lewis and his driver.

I pulled over and stopped. Colonel Lewis was nervous. I didn't blame him at all. I always wore my sidearm when making the trip, but he and the driver had both forgotten to take weapons with them. I gave the driver my pistol and told him I would send back a wrecker to tow him to Long Binh. Lewis and I got into the jeep and headed off.

The week passed slowly. Jack Charles and I spent a lot of time preparing ourselves for the worst. If General Mapes decided in the Air Force's favor, there would be no appeal. His word would be final. No matter what was done later, without the processing building, Alpha would no longer be a pleasant, efficient place.

At last, the decision came through. General Martin gave us the news: General Mapes had vetoed the Air Force plan. Thank God!

Captain Black, my adjutant, came to me one day to tell me that he had been reviewing the Army Emergency Relief (AER) funds that we had been directed to pick up from units going home. I had been aware that the 90th was the dumping ground for these funds, but had not given it much thought. AER funds were used to give loans to people in need. In Vietnam they were usually given to GIs who were granted emergency leaves to the States so they could buy a plane ticket to get home from Travis Air Force Base. But what Jim Black told me that day really got my attention. He had reviewed the records of a division size unit that had gone home months ago. The loans given the troopers had never been repaid—$90,000 worth. And since the 90th was now the custodian of the fund, as CO, I was responsible for collecting the old debts. Some dated back years. Obviously, many of the people involved were no longer in the service. Jim had reviewed the books of only one unit. There were many others. On the whole, the books were a nightmare of incomplete and sloppy record-keeping.

We decided to send a letter to the division Commanding General, now stationed in the States, with a list of the people who owed money and the amounts. We weren't optimistic, but at least the ledgers would show that I had tried to get the money back.

"Has USARV been on our ass?" I asked Jim.

"I've tried to talk to various people, but without result. They don't seem very concerned—they don't want to be bothered. They've got enough to worry about."

Payday in the Army is the last day of the month. The finance people were in the process of installing a new automated pay system called JUMPS, already installed in most other Army commands worldwide. Vietnam was next. The conversion from the old to the new system had been delayed a few times, but the finance people finally took the plunge in late 1971. We got our payroll, and the uproar was immediate. Some soldiers received pay slips with no pay due, others got amounts ranging from $5 to

$10. My pay slip indicated $6. Everywhere, the question was the same, "How much did you get paid?"

Since I had to go up to see Lewis anyway, I thought I'd stop by the finance building to get things straightened out. When I approached the building, however, I saw that the 90th was not the only unit with problems. The field surrounding the building on three sides was full of every type of military vehicle, including an armored personnel carrier. I found a spot to park and went in. It was bedlam. The reception area was packed. Harried clerks were trying their best to answer questions. It would be hours before I reached the counter.

I went next door and called Jim Black. He said he would get our finance clerk and pay records out of the finance center after it closed for the day. Then he'd bring both the clerk and the records to the battalion that night so the problems could be addressed in relative peace and quiet. And that's how it was. All that evening and into the night, people of the 90th entered my Headquarters building to correct the pay errors.

The battalion had one gun jeep. It was a typical jeep with a gun mount welded onto the frame. On the mount we placed a .50-caliber machine gun. The vehicle belonged to the MPs and was used to lead bus convoys to and from the airport. The jeep itself was unstable. Adding the weight of the gun mount and weapon had moved the center of gravity up even higher and made the vehicle almost impossible to drive safely. It was constantly in CWO Russo's motor pool for repairs to fenders, the windshield, and more.

CWO Russo was a genius for getting the parts and getting it back on the road, but he was constantly at odds with Joe Stanley and the MPs for their careless driving. One day, the convoy was just returning, led by the gun jeep. It had recently been rebuilt and had a new coat of bright shiny paint. After the jeep entered the compound, the driver turned toward Headquarters Company. He cut the wheels too sharply and the jeep rolled over on its side. Its occupants were dumped out in the roadway. CWO Russo's face went white. He began to run toward the jeep.

His interest was not the vehicle. He wanted the driver. The driver, a six-foot-four, 235-pound PFC, saw the chief running toward him. He didn't want any part of Mr. Russo, so he got up and began to run toward his company's orderly room and the safety of Captain Stanley. Mr. Russo gave chase for 50 yards, calling the trooper every name he could think of. Then he walked back to the jeep.

The MPs at the gate were in the process of righting the jeep. Russo called them off. "Keep your fucking hands off. Not one of you MPs is worth a good fuck. My people will pick it up." And he turned to me.

"I'm worried about the MPs who were thrown out," I said.

"Don't worry about those dumb fuckers, Colonel. They all landed on their head. They couldn't possibly be hurt. I'm not fixing it this time. These guys fuck it up every time I fix it. No more! Fuck them!" He got into his jeep and headed toward the motor pool.

By this time Joe Stanley had arrived with the driver in tow. Joe was about to chew out his MPs for not getting the jeep off the roadway. But I broke in: "The chief will do it, Joe. If any of your people touch it, he'll kill them, and he's mad enough to do it."

I told Joe what the chief had said about not repairing it and suggested he not bring up the subject until the chief cooled down. But I also said I wanted the jeep back on the road as soon as possible. In the end, it took Joe two days, a couple of cases of beer, and a lot of cajoling to get Russo to finally start repairs. The vehicle was back on the road in about a week.

The bus drivers presented another problem. They were "juicers." Their drinking feats were legend. When they were instructed to give their urine samples along with the members of the 90th Replacement Battalion, all the permanent-party soldiers were calling out, "No heads in that group—but if they're measured for beer content, they are in trouble."

The platoon belonged to the transportation brigade but was housed on my compound. The buses were Japanese-made and had been issued to the brigade during my first week in the battalion, replacements for the old US-made ones. Within four months, the buses were unrecognizable: scratches on the sides, dents, and broken windows. But never an accident. The drivers loved to push them as fast as they would go. That's why it was important to have the gun jeep leading them—not so much for protection, but to slow down the pace. The bus drivers were always plotting ways to get ahead of the gun jeep.

One day I received a call from the USARV Provost Marshall, a one-star general. He was absolutely beside himself, yelling so loud that at first I couldn't understand a word he was saying.

"The bus drivers have just forced me off the roadway and into a rice paddy." Seems he was headed to the airport, and the buses were on their way back. They were well over the middle of the roadway, and the only choice his driver had was to take to the paddy.

"Campbell, what in hell are you going to do about this?"

"I'll investigate sir and get back with you."

After a few choice words, he hung up.

I called Colonel Ed Phillips, the brigade commander. Before I could tell him what had happened, he said, "I know, I know, the PM has just gotten off the phone." Phillips was sending a major down to investigate. In about an hour the major came into my office. I had gone through the Infantry Basic Officers Course with him many years before.

"I want to get the story," he said.

"Well, something has to be done to calm the drivers down," I said. "How about bringing some new people in and moving others out to Long Binh?"

"But every time I send a new man down, he invariably picks up the habits of the platoon," he argued.

"Maybe a new NCO would help," I suggested.

Right after he left, I got calls from Lewis, Wagner, and even General Martin—the same old saw, "Don't do that again!" After the major reported his findings, the bottom line was that the convoy was exceeding the speed limit. The lead driver was given an Article 15, and a new NCO was transferred to command the platoon.

Toward the last part of 1971, American strength fell to 156,000. More and more units were standing down. Because of this reduction, the army now found itself overstaffed with helicopter pilots. During the height of the war, the schools were putting out thousands of new pilots each year. Most were given the rank of warrant officer. But now there was a surplus and the army couldn't absorb all the pilots back in the States, so many young WOs were given ninety days' notice that their services were no longer needed.

They began to appear at the battalion. Sometimes a group of thirty would appear all at once, none of them happy. They took up residence in the officer's club bar. They were fun-loving and didn't do anything serious, but they did drive my MPs crazy—with small things like running through the officers' barracks and waking everyone up. The complaints would hit my desk the next day.

The drug program had become routine. But even though the roving teams were still in operation, we were still picking up 6 to 7 percent of the returnees for a trip to the detox.

Around Thanksgiving, Fred Myers went off on R&R to Hawaii. One evening, Connie and I were feeling sorry for ourselves because we had not been off the compound in over a week. I had a rule that one of the three of us had to be on the compound at all times. We both wanted a steak in the worst way. The officers' club in the next unit over from us always had great ones, so I decided it would be okay to go over and get one. We would only be gone an hour. So, telling the duty officer where we would be, we got into

Connie's jeep and drove over. The meal satisfied a craving, but we didn't linger. We came right back to the compound.

When we entered the back gate, we could see a large crowd outside the NCO club. Connie floored it. The duty officer spotted us and came running. There had been an argument inside and it turned into a brawl—black against white. He was about to turn the MPs loose. I said no. Connie and I began to walk among the troopers, telling them to move off and get some sleep. But their mood was ugly. We persisted, and finally some began to move toward the barracks.

When a scuffle broke out at the door, the security platoon leader was on the two guys immediately. He pushed them back inside the club, which was now almost empty. A few of my NCOs began to appear and walk amongst the seething men. Talking all the time, each NCO kept breaking the group into smaller and smaller groups, and the heat of the situation began to cool. After about an hour, the area was completely clear. The club was a mess, but nothing serious. I put the MPs on alert for the night, but put no more on guard than usual.

Connie and I got back to Headquarters, dropped into chairs, and looked at one another. It had been close—it could have turned into a full-fledged riot. This had happened at the 22nd Replacement Battalion at Cam Rhan Bay when the commander was away. To defuse the brawl, someone had thrown a smoke grenade into the club. That really got things going. The poor bastard was still answering questions.

I told Connie, "The next time I suggest something against the rules, tell me to go to hell."

Before we'd recovered, the duty officer was yelling for us—there was a fire in the 381st. I could see the flames out my window. Connie ran for his jeep and I for mine. Connie headed for the motor pool to get our water trailer, but the duty officer had already called the Long Binh fire department. I headed straight for the 381st. The CO met me in the company street and said the furnace in the shower room had exploded. No one had been in the shower room at the time.

We had people fighting the fire with hand-held fire extinguishers, but it was getting away from them. A crowd gathered. Everyone had come out of the officers' club, and the MPs were beginning to push them back. Connie arrived with Mr. Russo and some of his crew and the 10,000 gallon water trailer. They immediately went into action. Within seconds, water was gushing directly on the fire and soon it was out—just about this time the Vietnamese-manned fire trucks arrived from Long Binh. Along with them was the post commander, Bill Sonners.

Colonel Sonners came up to me to see if the fire department's services were needed, but he realized we had it under control. The crowd started to break up. Those who had emerged from the club quickly returned. Colonel Sonners said, "Tough day." He had also heard about the bus driver's encounter with the PM. As we stood talking, Mr. Russo started to back the water trailer onto the main roadway. He overshot the edge, and both back axles went into the swamp. Try as he might, he couldn't budge it. The only thing to do was to release all the remaining water in the trailer. Then he put the truck in gear and pulled free. As he turned the steering wheel, the truck was pointed ahead on the macadam roadway. I was standing behind. As the wheels released, clumps of mud shot out from between the dual wheels, covering me.

I could feel that everyone around me thought it was funny. But nobody would look at me. They were covering their faces and looking away. I started to laugh. Then everyone did.

Inspection of the officers' shower the next morning revealed that we had only lost half the building. People in the good end were taking cold showers. That day a new heater appeared. I didn't ask where it came from. Two days later, carpenters had the burned end of the building repaired. I didn't ask where the lumber came from, either.

Late one evening I was in my office finishing up some paperwork. Fred was on R&R and I had a bigger stack than usual. Even in a war zone, everything was done in triplicate. Just to get bulbs for our 16mm movie projectors required numerous copies of forms. At about 2200 hours, my phone rang.

The voice on the other end did not identify itself: "Make sure the troopers going out on the 1200 plane tomorrow are really shaped up." The phone went dead. What was the voice trying to tell me? Sitting back in my chair, I began to think about what could possibly be special about tomorrow's flight. I was getting nowhere, so I decided to go to the processing shack. The flight had been manifested a few hours ago. Maybe if I looked over the manifest, it would reveal something.

I asked the NCO for the manifest. Scanning the list, I saw nothing special. The ranking officer was a major. But the total caught my eye—248. That was an odd number.

I asked the NCO, "How many seats on this type of plane?"

He answered, "Two hundred fifty."

"Why did you go two short?"

"Received a call from a colonel in DCSLOG to book only 248."

"Didn't that seem off to you? They always want us to overbook to make sure all seats are full."

"Yes, but then I got busy and never gave it another thought."

My mind was racing. This was one of our few East Coast planes. Who could be going back to McGuire base on the East Coast? I remembered that while I was up at USARV that morning, someone said that Mrs. McDowell was in the country. Most generals had their wives in Bangkok or the Philippines, because their tours were usually long ones—two years or more.

"When is the Army/Navy football game?" I asked.

He looked at me rather strangely. "Next Saturday," he said.

I had the answer. It was General and Mrs. McDowell who would fill those two vacant seats. I said it aloud and the NCO asked how I was so sure.

The Army World-Wide Commander Conference always took place around the time of the game. If the Russians ever wanted to start a war, it would be to their advantage to fire the first shot at halftime of the Army/Navy game.

The CO of the 259th, Captain Jackson, was surprised to see

me when he answered my knock on the door of his hooch. I told him about the general. I told him I wanted the people on the flight formed up an hour earlier than usual and that I would personally inspect each trooper.

The next morning Jackson had the troops turned out in khaki and lined up in formation. I stepped in front and ordered them to attention. I gave the command to open ranks march and then put them at ease. I began in the front rank. The processing NCOs followed behind me. They were equipped with shoe polish, blitz cloths for brass, and scissors. The usual bitching took place, but the worst was reserved for times when I told a man his mustache would have to be trimmed.

If he complained too much, I would ask, "Do you want to go home on this plane?" That seemed to put things in perspective.

After my inspection, we loaded the buses and I jumped into the lead vehicle for the convoy to the airport. We offloaded and sat the men down in the terminal. The bird was ready, but General McDowell was nowhere in sight. I turned my attention to the VIP room—a tiny cubicle containing two chairs and a table on which there was a coffee pot and some ancient magazines. I had the inappropriate magazines disposed of, and the sergeant made some coffee.

I walked to the roadway side of the terminal, fully expecting McDowell to pull up in a sedan. Still no show. Then in the distance I heard the distinctive sound of an approaching helicopter. He was coming in on the other side. I rushed to the airfield side, arriving just as the copter was setting down.

After a few moments, the general and his wife came down the steps, followed by an aide.

McDowell walked up to me, said good morning, and returned my salute. He introduced me to his wife, and the aide and I exchanged stiff smiles. This was the same guy who had discovered the beer in my steam bath. I accompanied them to the VIP suite and left them. The Air Force major behind the counter beckoned to me. The plane had engine trouble and would be delayed.

"How long?" I asked. He didn't know. I said, "Why me, God?"

The major gave me a strange look. I spoke to McDowell's aide, who was standing outside the VIP room. He disappeared inside to tell the general. McDowell came out and I delivered the bad news.

He turned to go back, but stopped and turned to me and said, "It's lunchtime. How are you going to feed the troopers?" I smiled to myself. I was finally a step ahead. We had a container at the terminal full of C-rations for just such emergencies.

I turned to one of the NCOs and said, "Break out the C's." In a matter of minutes the people started to distribute the chow. I turned to General McDowell and asked if he and Mrs. McDowell would care to partake. He turned to the aide.

"Get a sedan. We're going to the club for lunch."

By 1500, the plane was finally ready. I sure was thankful to whoever had tipped me off.

An article appeared in the *Overseas Weekly*, a newspaper published for Americans. The troops referred to it as the "Oversexed Weekly" because of its pictures. A front page article accused me and the people of the 90th of lowering the morale by forcing men to wear baseball caps rather than their unit's distinctive headgear. The article quoted the Sergeant Major of the 1st Cavalry Division.

About this time a unit of the 1st squadron of the 9th Cavalry was standing down and being re-formed in the States. This group could trace its lineage back to frontier days. It was a helicopter unit—but not your ordinary helicopter unit. These guys flew attack helicopters over VC territory, exposing themselves in order to attract enemy fire. It was a harrowing job, and men of the 9th wore brown cowboy hats as a badge of honor. We got the word that a group of them would be processing through the 90th and would be carrying their unit colors.

The unit commander sent an NCO over a day before to make the arrangements for the colors and the men. He arrived wearing his cowboy hat. But after a short conversation with Captain Jackson, he agreed to switch to the baseball cap. That evening, however, he and one of my NCOs had a fistfight. The man from the Cav unit came off second-best and had a beautiful black eye the next morning.

The men of the 1st of the 9th arrived together late that afternoon. All were wearing cowboy hats. I had someone look up the commander and get him to my office. But even before he appeared, my people started to report some of the statements attributed to these men; they were here and they wanted trouble. The NCO with the black eye was fueling the fire.

The major arrived at my office and rendered a very snappy salute.

"Your people will have to obey my rules," I told him. "The incident between the two NCOs was unfortunate, but it can't generate any further disturbance—it could erupt into a full-scale riot."

"I'll have my men change their hats," he agreed, "but I can't guarantee calm. We've been out in the bush a long time. The enemy's elusiveness has worn their nerves thin, and they've wanted a good standup fistfight."

I said, "If that is the case, major, I want you in this office at 1930." He looked puzzled. "You and I are going to be seen together all evening and night long. You'll accompany me on my nightly rounds."

At 1930, the major appeared and we set out. There had been no trouble during the afternoon. We started with the steam bath. A few of his troopers were there, but all seemed peaceful. They were enjoying themselves. Mr. Kim said that there had been no incidents during the day. The same story at the snack bar. Next we went to the NCO/EM club. If there was to be trouble, it would probably start there.

A large group of people gathered one corner. One of them stood up and motioned the major and me over. As we approached, it became obvious that the group was made up of both 1st Cav and 90th people. At the center were the two NCOs who had fought the night before, now buddies. The sergeant major insisted we sit with them and have a beer. The group was friendly and the Cav people were telling war stories.

After a short time, I was paged over the loudspeaker system. The officers' club sergeant wanted to speak to me. I picked up the phone. There were loud noises in the background at the other end.

The club sergeant said, "There are eight officers with cowboy hats on."

"Are they buying a round of drinks for the house?" I asked. It's an army tradition—anyone who enters a bar with headgear on must buy everyone a drink.

"Yeah, they're buying for everyone all night. They've put $100 on the bar, and they said when it ran out, to let them know."

"You have no bitch," I retorted, and hung up.

The next day the group boarded the buses for the airport. As the last one left, one of the Cav troopers flew a sheet out the back. On it was painted, "Thanks 90th." That made me feel good.

About 0100 on December 2nd,1971 the phone rang at my bedside. It was the major from USARV Headquarters who handled assignments for the Army's colonels. His day started at midnight because of the time difference between Vietnam and the Pentagon.

He said, "I have the following message for you from Washington: 'The book has been published and your name is in it.' End of message. What did the message mean?" I couldn't tell him without getting someone in trouble. The promotion board list had just been run on the computer, and I had been selected for promotion to colonel. The lists were kept secret until publication, but a friend had passed me the word beforehand. At times, there were advantages to being in the technical community.

I jumped out of bed, picked up a bottle of scotch, and still in my shorts, ran across to the trailer that housed Fred and Connie. I pounded on the door. Connie answered, expecting another crisis. When I told both the news, they were happy for me. But I don't believe they enjoyed the forced drink at 0130 in the morning. If I could only make it through the rest of my tour without getting relieved of my command, I would get the promotion.

Colonel Wagner, the AG, called. "I noticed that the beer-in-the-steam-bath case is no longer on the general's calendar."

"What happened?" I asked.

"Don't know," he said. "Looks like he dropped it."

I could hardly believe all this good news. But as things seemed to go with the 90th, you seldom, if ever, stayed on a lucky roll. As I stepped out the front door, I noticed a lowboy truck coming up the street. It was loaded with big crates, stacked too high to pass under the communication lines running from the Tactical Operation Center to the front-line watchtowers. Waving my arms, I started to run toward the truck. It stopped, but too late. The top crate had completely severed all the communication lines.

"Oh, shit!" Over the years, as one line went dead, others were strung parallel to the old, useless wires. I once remarked to the communications sergeant that he should cut down the excess. He said it was too dangerous. Some of that stuff had been up for years. It was like a bowl of spaghetti—impossible to separate the good from the bad.

When the communications sergeant arrived on the scene, I said, "Here's your chance to clean up this mess."

"I can," he acknowledged, "but it will take longer to get back in contact with the watchtower if I clean up the old wire first."

I said, "Run lines on the ground up to the watchtowers. Then clean up the mess. When that's done, put the live wires on the pole." In a couple of days, the spaghetti bowl was gone.

The pump broke, forcing us to close the pool. The men wanted to swim in it anyway, and some would even climb over the fence. I had to post a guard. It would take us four days to drain the pool and clean it, and six more to fabricate the part to get the pump working again. In the meantime, the medics visited and put an off-limits sign on the pool. Then they wrote me up for insufficient square footage around the bunks in the barracks. Didn't these staff guys have anything better to do? The buildings, with the same number of bunks, had been here for nearly six years.

Next, we had our second fire. It started at the drop point where the returnees disposed of their jungle fatigues, boots, and whatever other clothing they didn't want. The quartermaster outfit was to pick it up for salvage. However, because of short staffing, their pickups became more and more infrequent. One day the pile just burst into flames. When the flames were out, I had a detail of returnees shovel the rank garments into trucks.

Naturally, in the middle of the cleanup, General McDowell showed up. This time USARV Sergeant Major McGiff was with him.

"You should not let this stuff pile up," said McDowell. Then he spotted two GIs without headgear and, of course, made his favorite comment: "These men are yours. Get them shaped up." Next he decided to go into the PX. The sergeant major was going to follow, but I grabbed his arm and motioned him to stay with me. Sergeant McGiff was built like a wrestler—short, bull-chested, and with legs like a fullback's.

I asked him, "What's with the old man? He's always on my ass!"

"He likes you," McGiff said.

I said, "He what?"

"He thinks you're doing a good job."

"I don't believe it."

"Listen, I've been with him while he inspected other battalions. I've seen him make an entire tour without saying a word. When he got back to his sedan, he relieved the commander on the spot. As long as he keeps on your ass, you're doing okay. If he clams up on you, you're in trouble."

The general came out with a small package, gave us both a funny look, and motioned the sergeant major into the sedan. Just as the general was getting in the car, he turned to me: "Come on, get in and we'll go up to see how things are at the detox center."

I thought, the last time I took a ride with a general up there, I had to walk back.

He said, "Don't worry, I'll give you a ride back." The man was incredible. Was it possible he could read my mind? When I was a kid, I had always thought telepathy was the special talent of fathers.

As I got in the back seat, a big dog jumped on my lap—a mixed breed, but more Labrador than anything else.

"He's very tame," said the general. "He just wants to play." All the way up to the center, this damn dog was all over me. He knocked off my cap and stepped on my balls about three times. I thought, this is the man who said I had too many dogs.

These were strange times in the Army. It was the beginning of the long-hair phase, of mustaches, and peace symbols. The regulations on hair length and mustache size were subject to differing interpretations. On one side, the troopers would stretch the rule as far as they could. On the other side, older NCOs and officers would push it the other way. The peace symbol was the first thing banned, then approved for wear around the neck, as long as it was kept inside the shirt. Trying to enforce these rules was almost impossible, so I tried to be lenient.

One day, the officers of the 381st were throwing a football around in the street. The young lieutenant on duty behind the reception counter was part of the game. He always wore a peace symbol, which didn't bother me. (In fact, a year earlier, I had tried to sell the idea of the symbol to my boss as a recruiting poster and almost lost my head. By now, that same poster was now seen throughout USARV.) In a case of poor timing, a captain who was on his way back to the States came along to sign in, and the lieutenant left the game and ducked in behind the counter to give the captain the necessary forms. The captain noticed the peace symbol and began to chew him out. The company commander intervened and cooled the captain down. But during his stay, he made it a point to harass the lieutenant.

I was totally unaware that this was happening. Connie had cut the captain off from seeing me on two occasions. As I learned later, the captain opted to go on an East Coast flight. He was manifested for it, but his baggage went to the West Coast. And before he left, the MPs at the airport decided to single him out for a strip search. I often wondered at what point he came to realize that he had messed with the wrong people.

Someone came up with a case of chicken, so all the officers gathered at my trailer area for a barbecue. CWO Campbell was gone—I did the cooking. I had just finished and sat down to eat. As I was raising a chicken leg up to my mouth, there was the sound of machine gun fire from the direction of the front wire. I dropped the chicken and began to run for my jeep. Joe Stanley was already heading for the front gate. As we approached the MP, he was pointing up toward Headquarters Company.

The firing had come from one of our watchtowers. The guard was scared shitless. He had been placing the M-60 machine gun up on its stand, which was the procedure as night came on. But as he was loading it, he had kept his finger on the trigger. The empty brass casings showed that six rounds had been fired. But where did they land? The village across the road was filled with Vietnamese. I took my jeep across Route 1 and drove every back street in the area. There was no indication that anyone or anything had been hit. After about an hour, I returned to my cold chicken. God had been good to me once again.

Christmas was fast approaching, which meant busy times for us. Army tradition holds that people with DEROS close to the 25th get sent back in time for the holiday. This year, anyone due back in the States by December 28th would be home by the 24th. Of course, this put extra pressure on the majors in the AG and DCSLOC to come up with enough planes. I was planning to go back to Hawaii for R&R on the 24th.

The crush of people began on the 20th. We were processing six planes a day out of Bien Hoa. Captain Hardee, who had become all but a member of the 90th by his frequent visits with TV crews and newspaper reporters, came in on the 23rd. But the next morning, we manifested the last flight out until the 28th of December—he was one of about thirty people that didn't make the plane. I felt bad for him because of the protection he had offered us. But he didn't complain. He would live in the S-1 and S-4 trailer while he waited for a seat home.

I left Long Binh for Alpha, destined for the noon 747 out of Tan Son Nhut. I was met by Major Charles and one of the Pan Am representatives, Bud Tate. Bud told me he had a surprise for me— I was going home in the first class cabin.

"I can't," I protested. The government had contracted only for the back of the plane.

He looked at me and said, "Whose airplane is it, anyway?" He wouldn't take no for an answer. So I agreed.

I was back in Hawaii nearly three days before I could begin to relax. I knew in a few short days, I would be heading back to Vietnam. But at least when I got there, it would be 1972, the year I would rotate.

CHAPTER 8
VIETNAMIZATION

Vietnamization was the term coined to show that the Americans were leaving country and turning the war over to those who should rightly fight it—the Vietnamese. We had made over the Vietnamese Army into our image: big divisions with tanks and heavy artillery, officer efficiency reports to ensure the best officers were promoted and to eliminate politics, and a personnel system that was a duplicate of the American Army's—including the paperwork. There was even a morning report from every unit, so that a computer in Saigon could keep track of the army's strength. Uniforms, weapons, and helmets all were the same as ours. Our political leaders were advertising that we had done as much as we could for the Vietnamese, and now it was their turn to defend their homeland. We were going to have "Peace with Honor."

The average soldier who had served in Vietnam and been exposed to ARVN did not quite believe that the Vietnamese were—or would ever be—ready to defend their homeland. He just wanted to leave this saddest of places.

By January 1972, the 90th was beginning to process more and more returnees and fewer and fewer replacements. The groups carrying unit colors home increased. But to reduce the strength as quickly as we had been directed, the 90th now began to out-

161

process people who had just arrived. Some people were getting "drops" from their normal twelve-month tours. Others were ordered home after only six months in country—a new phenomenon that affected the morale of the people assigned to the 90th.

In February, I closed down the 18th Enlisted Replacement Company. Some of the people were reassigned to the 259th Returnee Company to assist with their ever-increasing workload. Likewise, during my trips to USARV Headquarters, I could see what the reduction in strength was doing to the population of Long Binh. Some of the barracks were completely deserted, giving the area the look of a ghost town.

During the first three months of 1972, we constantly had to come up with different plans in response to directions coming from Headquarters. The first directive declared that strength, by late spring, would be down to 100,000 and that Long Binh would be shrunk. The outer east wire of the 90th would be the eastern end of Long Binh. Swell, I thought, now I can defend two sides of the compound.

The first change was not long in coming. The battalion area would be cut in half and new wire laid down the main battalion street. The battalion would be operated from the southern side of the wire, and the buildings north of the street would be destroyed. This involved the loss of two of the three mess halls, leaving only the smallest to support both officers and enlisted people. The plan stood for a while. In fact, the engineers began to stock barbed wire to do the job.

Mr. Kim's steam bath contract was not renewed. Many of the

vendors, who were third-country nationals, were let go after their employment contracts expired. The objective was to let Vietnamese businesspeople get the contracts, instead. Mr. Kim was angry as hell. He protested bitterly to me and took his case up the line. On his last day, he took sledge hammers to the walls. When I found out, I complained to the USARV. I was told Mr. Kim had built the building with his own funds and could do anything he wished. After he departed, we had padlocks put on the doors.

The next contract to expire was the barbershop's. It seemed that another Vietnamese had underbid the present Vietnamese manager. But in this case, the building belonged to the American government. I sent Fred up to the shop on the day it was to change hands. Much to his chagrin, the old barbers were in the process of breaking up the place, while some of the new barbers were fighting with a rear guard of the old ones. The two managers were yelling and screaming at one another. Fred called the MP patrol, and after a while, he managed to separate the two groups. He accompanied the outgoing group to the front gate, where he and the MPs picked up their passes.

When told about the fracas, I walked up to see if the shop could operate. When I arrived, some people were busy picking up the place, and others were already cutting hair. The manager stepped forward. She was one of the most beautiful Vietnamese women I had ever seen.

"Everything will be in order by day's end," she assured me. "This is not my only contract with the Americans. I managed all the other barbershops on Long Binh. I will bring equipment from my other shops to replace the broken ones." She was so businesslike, I felt reassured.

That night, while making my rounds in the battalion area, I was walking past the darkened PX when someone stepped out of the shadows. It was An, the barbershop manager. Angry, I told her to never do that again and that she shouldn't be walking around the area at night by herself. I didn't know if she understood the implications of my second remark.

She had a sack in her hand. "I have the day's receipts to give to Mr. Ono. But Mr. Ono is gone for the day. What do I do with the money?"

I thought, a beautiful woman with a sack of money—how much more trouble could she be looking for? "Follow me," I said. "I'll lock it in my safe until tomorrow." In my office, I noticed she had the beginnings of a black eye and was scratched on her neck and head.

"When I go home at lunch time, the old manager and barbers take me."

"How are you going to get home tonight?"

"My brother will meet me at the front gate." He was an ARVN soldier stationed in Bien Hoa.

I drove her to the front gate in my jeep and asked her to stay inside the fence while I checked for her brother. As I looked up and down the roadway, I noticed a car about 100 yards up the road. When the driver saw me come out, he began to drive toward me. Out of each window pointed a M-16 rifle. I was terrified for a moment, sure it was the VC and that my ass was grass. But it was her brother with his military friends.

A new figure for American troop strength was announced: 69,000 by April 30th. That meant the 90th was going to be a madhouse. Furthermore, because of the precipitous drop in strength, the battalion would no longer remain at Long Binh. In fact, we would close down all the companies at Long Binh and process everyone through the 178th at Camp Alpha—it was going to become the entire replacement battalion for all of Vietnam—beginning April 30th.

On April 1st, all replacements would be processed through Camp Alpha. Thank God for General Mape's decision to allow the Army to hold on to the processing building there. The new plan called for new wire to be erected down the battalion's main street, which would become the north boundary of Long Binh, and for the destruction of all the buildings on the compound. The demolition west of the wire would allow for the construction of fortifications to protect what remained.

During March, we began to move all the CIF stock to Camp Alpha. This done, we closed up another building. We also began to reopen all the 18th Replacement barracks we had earlier closed to get ready for the number of returnees we were going to process. We even drew more beds and mattresses from the depot. The battalion was now capable of sleeping approximately 3,200 people per night. I thought about reopening the 18th Company mess, but decided against it. We didn't have enough cooks and we had turned in much of the kitchen equipment. There was no hope of getting any more cooks or of having the kitchen equipment back from the depot in time to do any good.

The AG and DCSLOG staff were working day and night to figure out how many planes would be required to lift people out. When I got a look at the numbers, I was worried. Could we process that many? On some days, during the middle of the month, we were going to be processing twelve plane loads a day—3,600 people. Some of the same questions we had at the beginning of the drug program were being asked once again. Could the medics keep up with the processing? Would we have enough people to fill the planes? The pace of the withdrawal was insane. Washington insisted that American military strength be no more than 69,000 troopers—not even one more. People at Headquarters suggested that if we did not make that level by the end of the month, the world would end.

If we were to process twelve planes on some days, that meant the population sometimes would exceed the number of beds we had. This didn't bother me too much. I had seen returnees for almost a year now. Many never went near their bunk. Some were so worked up over going home, they would roam about all night or spend time just bullshitting with other GIs. Some of the combat unit soldiers still worried about mortar attacks and were too nervous to sleep in a building. Others would rather take their chances sleeping on the ground away from the populated areas.

To get the strength down, many more individuals would get drops. The rules published for figuring out your new DEROS were mind-boggling. Initially, I assumed the people assigned to the 90th would be exempt from the drop policy—we had too much to accomplish. The directive, though, said all units in Vietnam would fall under the drop program. No amount of persuasion could sway Lewis.

The 90th also faced the problem of securing the compound. Since the replacements had dwindled to a trickle, our security platoon was shorthanded. I asked if we could at least keep the men we had; the request went unheeded. By mid-April, all the transients now in the platoon would be assigned line units, and the watchtowers would be manned by my MPs. But by the end of April, their ranks would also shrink because of the drop program.

At the middle of March I called together the staff and company commanders to discuss the looming dilemma. Jim Black pointed out that during April, battalion strength would fall by over 60 percent. All the officers volunteered to stay until the end and go out on the last plane. They assured me that the NCOs would also volunteer to stay. I appreciated their loyalty. We figured that the processing people would continue working twelve-hour shifts, but that by mid-month, we would be booking two planes simultaneously. As a result, the workday might extend to twenty hours.

The S-4, Lieutenant Andy Worth, was ordering additional rations for the mess halls, additional sheets, and extra "asswipes," the Army's term for toilet paper. Mr. Ono, due to leave at any moment, was invited to the meeting and brought his replacement along. I was sorry to see him go—he was the best PX manager I had ever seen. His stock was unmatched anywhere outside the US. He assured me that he'd ordered more than double his usual inventory of soda. It was an important commodity as we entered the dry season, when the temperature could rise to 110 degrees. Even as time dulls my memory of Vietnam, the one thing I will always remember is how hot it was and how uncomfortable I was while there. Mr. Ono had also stocked up on campaign ribbons, for no matter how much a man hated Vietnam, when he left, he would always be wearing his ribbons.

In an attempt to get rid of everything that would not be useful in the last month, Lieutenant Worth tried to turn in the books in our library. He met with a shock. USARV said they could not handle any more, and that we should give them away. That afternoon, we gave dibs to members of the 90th. Then we opened the library to the transients with a sign that read, "Take all you want, but read all you take." A variation of that sign appeared in every mess hall in the Army.

Lewis got a drop notice—he was due to go home six weeks before DEROS. The lieutenant colonel taking over his position called me that afternoon with a request: the AG was planning to recommend Lewis for the Legion of Merit, and would like me to contribute to Lewis's write-up. I told his replacement that Lewis hadn't been inside the compound in six months. He repeated that the AG still wanted me to contribute. Remembering our fallout, I gave the assignment to Fred.

The new PX manager came to my office in a state of shock. That morning, when he went to his safe to get yesterday's receipts to deliver to the bank—$20,000 worth of scrip—he found nothing but cut up pieces of paper.

"Does anyone else have the combination to the safe?" I asked.

"No, only me." It had been changed the day before.

"Can you explain the loss?"

"Well," he said, "I had two Vietnamese helping me, as usual. As I was about to put the bag into the safe, one of them distracted me for a moment. It must have been long enough for the other to pull a switch." He was picturing his career with the exchange system going down the drain.

"Did either of them report to work today?"

"No," he answered.

"Report this immediately to your superiors in USARV," I said. About a week later, both women were caught, but no money was found. The manager got off with a letter of reprimand.

The AG reassigned Connie Johnson to Alpha to help Major Charles set up the procedures there. This was a loss. Connie was a good soldier who'd made my command a lot easier. Nevertheless, I could not fault the AG. He had to ensure that Alpha was ready to carry on after April 30th. Colonel Wagner told me that Connie would go to Alpha, and said all he wanted me to do was to get through April and close down the battalion at Long Binh. Then, I could go home early. That was the carrot. If I were lucky, I could possibly get out fifteen days early. Major Charles would also be rotating in a few months, and he was putting another lieutenant colonel in command of Alpha. The new one was due in mid-June. I told Colonel Wagner that Connie would be fine running Alpha by himself, but the colonel still insisted the new man be brought in.

The first few days in April passed without an appreciable increase in the returnee population. The staff was like a well-prepared football team awaiting the start of the big game. The day Connie departed for Alpha, however, the game began. The first day, we processed over 2,000 men. The line outside the pee house was backed up to the front gate. Mercifully, the men's attitudes were cheerful—after all, many were going home long before they had expected to. The medics kept up with the turnaround and cleared enough people to fill all the airplanes' seats. The next day, another 2,000 people showed up, and the population by that night rose to about 3,000. At this point, everyone still had a bunk. The mess halls were busy but not overcrowded. The snack bar was doing a hell of a business, though, and so were the kitchens in both clubs and the stand outside the PX. The pool was overcrowded, and the PX was so full that the manager had to close the door at times to keep the crowd inside to a manageable size. We manifested seven planes that day.

The next day, 2,000 more people entered. This rate continued for a week, and then the workload became even heavier. We were out of bunks and under pressure to keep enough food in the snack bar. Because of the heat, we were already running out of soda. The battalion area was wall-to-wall with people. I had never seen so many transients. Many were candidates for detox.

People assigned to the battalion were also departing at a rapid rate, creating other problems. It was becoming more and more difficult to secure the front bunker line. The battle of An Loc had broken out about 40 kilometers from us. The reports we were receiving suggested it was touch-and-go. If the ARVN were incapable of holding on, the enemy would soon be at our front door. This concern forced me once again to ask for replacements to man the security platoon. A forty-one-man over strength was authorized, and men were assigned from the replacement pool to the battalion.

I wasn't the only one worried. One day, I received a call from a colonel at USARV. He said that the DCSOPS were concerned about the problem, and it had come up at General McDowell's staff meeting. The solution was to issue me 800 M-16 rifles. I was to hand out to the transients in case of an emergency.

It was so ludicrous that I began to laugh. The colonel was surprised. He asked what was so funny. I answered that if there was an emergency, all the transients would "di" (Vietnamese for "bug out") for the security of Long Binh. Having gotten this far, they felt as though they were already home. The mental toughness that kept them alive in the bush was gone.

The colonel could not see my point. "The weapons will be delivered tomorrow." He hung up.

Four big crates arrived, each containing 200 M-16 rifles. The weapons were coated with Cosmoline, a gelatinous semi-solid, and still in their factory wrappings. I told the S-4 to store them in one of our now-empty Quonset huts. One small lock protected them. This was hardly up to regulation, but I simply didn't have the space to secure them.

The medics doing the urinalysis were working about twenty hours a day. The pee house was sometimes kept open for eighteen hours. The line was always a quarter mile long. Things still worked. We booked as many as twelve flights in a single day. But the processing guys were dead on their feet.

One day as I was walking through the area, I felt a tug at my elbow. I saw the smiling face of a major. He asked if I remembered him. I looked at his name tag, but that was no help.

"Sorry, I don't. Should I?"

"I'm the person who called you about your 105 Howitzer." The thing was still around—just as it had always been. "I filled out the paperwork for you and that's why the weapon is still onsite."

"Thanks," I said, and moved on. I couldn't believe the Army had wasted a major's efforts in this manner, and he probably had a staff to help him.

The next unexpected piece of news was that the battalion buildings were not going to be demolished. The place would be turned over to a civilian engineering contracting firm that would use it to house their workers. Everything in the battalion would be given to them.

I told the S-4 about the change in plans, but not to worry about it now. "Get some trucks and help the PX get some more soda."

The crowds continued to pour in while the strength of the 90th continued to leak away. One morning late in the month, Captain Jackson and his first sergeant conducted police call for more than 4,000 people. They were armed with battery-operated megaphones to make themselves heard, and they were trying to give the processing NCOs a few hours of much-needed sleep.

Captain Jackson entered one of the barracks to announce the formation, a voice from the far end announced, "No fucking way! I have only two days to go." After everyone else had filed outside, this one black enlisted man was still lying on his bunk, eyes closed. Captain Jackson walked up to him. He put the megaphone right up to the man's ear and shouted, "Now, fucker!" The man's feet barely touched the floor. He went right through the screen door, taking it completely off its hinges.

The medics made their monthly inspection. They wrote me up for a lack of sleeping space and for the filthiest pool in recorded history. I told Fred to pull our answer to last month's inspection out of the files and reuse it. I hoped either we or they would be long gone before anything would come of it.

One day, I received a call from General McDowell's aide.

"The general will make his formal inspection of the battalion on Thursday," the colonel announced.

"Are you pulling my leg?" I asked.

The colonel said, "I will repeat the message"—and he did. I still couldn't believe my ears. He added, "The general will arrive by helicopter and land on the pad at 1400 hours."

I broke in. The pad had been off-limits for years, had been used for other purposes, and was not safe. Like a machine, the colonel just repeated the last part of the message.

He said the uniform for the day would be khakis with low quarters. I hadn't worn that uniform since I returned from R&R. Once more, I tried to point out that the general was more than a little familiar with the battalion.

"The general has made it a point to formally visit each battalion under his command," the colonel replied. "Yours is the only one that has not been checked off his chart." Great, in the middle of the busiest time this battalion has ever known, we had to worry about a chart.

At the appointed time, the sergeant major and I showed up at the helicopter pad on the infamous walkway. We were both feeling hot and uncomfortable in our khakis, and we stood in the swirling wind of the helicopter as it approached. About 30 feet from the pad, the back blast from the props lifted the rubber matting into the air. Seeing the danger, the pilot quickly banked and took the bird up again. As it turned away, the matting was still in the air, and the blast from his prop pushed the water beneath into one big wave. I was right in front of the splash. Water saturated the front of my uniform, but left me bone-dry in the back.

The sergeant major had gotten a little wet, but nothing like me. I looked down at myself. I suppose I had been lucky; at least there was no mud. But if that fucking aide had some balls, he would have stopped General McDowell from coming in the first place. I called that colonel every name in the book and had a few choice comments about the general, as well.

Now the pilot had taken the chopper around again and was approaching from a different direction. He seemed to be okay this time. When I looked up, I could see General McDowell was undergoing an attack of high hilarity. I looked at the pilot and copilot, and they were also laughing. Now I was pissed.

The sergeant major said, "Take it easy, sir. It's too close to the end to blow it now." As General McDowell emerged, he was clearly having a hard time keeping a straight face. I walked up and gave a salute.

He said, "I've seen enough of your battalion here at Long Binh. Get on board and we will visit Alpha."

I thought, that's why he choppered in. The son of a bitch wanted to catch me off guard. I hoped the sergeant major had followed what had happened. If he had, Alpha would get some warning, but not much.

As I got in the chopper, I was surprised to see another general officer aboard. No one could speak over the sound of the blades, so I put on a headset. General McDowell introduced me to the new DCSPER, General Watson. General Martin had left the country for Hawaii a week before. In fact, that day I had received a letter from my wife telling me she had met him at church.

The trip was even shorter than usual, since three stars cut through the rest of the traffic. The time in the chopper had dried out my uniform, but it now looked as if I had slept in it.

Luckily, the sergeant major had gotten word to both Connie and Jack. Jack began the tour of the area, and I noted that General Watson had critical remarks about everything. I thought, if he doesn't like this place, wait until he visits the rest of the battalion. Our last stop was the joint Officer/EM club. It was about 1530 hours and the place was packed.

General Watson asked Charles, "Why don't you have two separate clubs? They shouldn't mix officers and enlisted ranks. And they shouldn't be serving liquor at all. This place should be turned into an ice cream parlor."

Charles, Connie, and I exchanged some desperate looks. There would be riots! General McDowell didn't say anything and kept on walking. I hoped that he wouldn't go along with the idea. We got back on the helicopter. All the way back to Long Binh, General Watson kept up his grating commentary. He didn't have one positive word to say. Neither General McDowell nor I had much to say. We landed outside USARV and General McDowell had his driver take me back to the battalion.

On the trip, I realized how deserted Long Binh was becoming. Once-crowded places had no traffic at all. More and more barracks were being closed. We were really coming to the end. I thought about General Watson. If he were to visit, I would be in for a bad time. By midday, the place invariably looked like a garbage heap. When Charlie Connell called and asked me to have dinner and a few drinks with him, I told him that if I had one drink, I would be drunk for a week.

That Saturday night, I was invited to a dinner given by the post commander. During the cocktail hour, I found myself standing close to General McDowell.

"General, when you visited the 90th last week, I noticed you were having a difficult time keeping a straight face."

He said, "Campbell, put yourself in the chopper and me on the ground—how fucking funny would that be?" I don't believe he agreed with General Watson ideas.

The next visit was from the USARV Inspector General. Usually, the IG arrived with a team of people who delved into every facet of an organization. But this inspection consisted of a single lieutenant colonel. The reduction in strength was affecting the staff as well as the line. He told me he realized we were closing this part of the battalion in a few weeks, and so he would just conduct an informal visit. He simply wanted to talk to me and walk around a little.

Amid his visit, it was obvious that the transient population just kept getting larger and larger. We were processing so quickly that people put on a detail would be manifested before the detail was finished. The clothing in the drop-off point grew to the size of a mountain. A call to the quartermaster outfit went unanswered because there was no one there. They were already processing through the 90th on their way home.

Somehow, the IG bastard found out about the 800 weapons secured by only a single Yale lock. He never said a word about it to me, but the next day he reported it at McDowell's staff meeting.

My phone rang off the cradle. The AG, General Watson, General Kelley—how could I not have secured those weapons? I offered to turn them in, but no one would hear of that. The AG, Colonel Wagner, arrived. I showed him where the weapons were stored and took him to my two arms rooms, demonstrating that there was no way I could properly secure 800 weapons I had not asked for.

Fortunately, the AG agreed. He told me, "Turn them in. I'll cover for you." My God, a reasonable man! I never heard about the matter again. I waited for the IG lieutenant colonel to process through so we could give him some special treatment, but he never showed up.

Sometimes, I would sit and wonder if everyone was out to get me. It seemed as if every staff element existed in hopes of crucifying me—not helping me, as the manual specified. But just as I would be feeling sorriest for myself, something positive would happen. Captain Black came in one day to report that USARV had said to turn in all the AER fund books 'as-is'. We had gotten no reply from any unit we had sent inquiries to, so the people at USARV said the records would probably be destroyed and the $90,000 in debt written off.

I told Fred and Captain Black to update the history of the unit from my takeover until April 30th, and also to write up the necessary documentation for a meritorious unit citation for the 90th. In my mind, this group deserved the award more than any other unit I had ever served in.

Lieutenant Worth grabbed me as I was walking past his building.

"We're running out of toilet paper."

I said, "No problem. Go over to the depot and get some."

"My people just got back from there. They're out."

"What?" If we didn't have toilet paper for this mob, we would be in trouble. I told Worth to come with me to the Headquarters building.

Fred was busy trying to close out the eleven different funds we maintained to pay the Vietnamese hooch maids, shit burners, and all the rest. These funds were in piasters, Vietnam's currency at the time. Fred had told me earlier that after meeting the last payroll we could destroy the fund books. Nobody at USARV wanted them. The truth of the matter was that no one was left to do anything with them. I asked if he had prepared the last payroll. He had.

"How much money is left?"

"About two hundred dollars."

I told Fred, "Give it to Lieutenant Worth."

And I told Worth, "Go to the PX and buy all the toilet paper you can." About three hours later, Lieutenant Worth returned with a deuce and a half (a two-and-a-half-ton truck) of the now-scarce commodity. It was enough to see us through to the end.

Eighteen months later, I'd be stationed in Washington, DC and a civilian programmer would approach me. He'd tell me how he was just back from Vietnam where he had been a programmer in the American Logistics Command. I'd tell him the story about running out of toilet paper, and then I'd learn of the epilogue.

During those days in 1972, the Americans were sending great quantities of equipment out of Vietnam, as well as bringing in weapons, tanks, and ammo for the Vietnamese. Most of the material leaving went to Okinawa, where we had a big logistics command. One day, a teletype came from the general in command of the Okinawa Logistics Command, General Mapes—the same general who had been so decisive about the Army keeping Camp Alpha. The message read, "If you continue shipping asswipes to this island, you will sink it." Because of a mix up in stock numbers, toilet paper was being forwarded to Okinawa just as fast as it arrived in Vietnam!

Returnees kept pouring into the battalion. For the first time, their attitude seemed better than that of our people. They were extremely happy about leaving earlier than expected, but people of the 90th seemed testy. They were bone-tired, and our numbers got fewer each day. Those who stayed had to pick up more of the workload. The MPs were doing an about face coming and going. They would get off guard duty to drive the gun jeep in the convoy out to the airport, and come back to patrol the area. I stopped internal patrols.

Meanwhile, the population at the detox center was growing each day. Its staff was also dwindling, as was the 90th's. General Watson arrived one afternoon. As he stepped from his sedan, he didn't even bother to return my salute. He launched into a tirade about the condition of the area. Looking around, I had to agree. There were many Coke cans lying about. The fifty-five-gallon drums that served as litter cans were overflowing.

"We police the area in the morning," I explained, "but I'm shorthanded. I can't spare the people during the day."

"Not good enough. Come up with a way to keep this place clean. It looks like a dump!"

Great, another helping hand from Headquarters. He viewed the processing area and the pee house, but had little to say. He entered the PX. By this time, the shelves were almost empty, but he was only interested in the area where the campaign ribbons were sold. He had overheard one GI complain about the lack of the Army commendation ribbons. He wanted to see the manager. We went into the back, where the manager was moving stock out of the storeroom.

"Why aren't you stocking a full inventory of ribbons?" asked the general. The response—that there were none in the depot— did not satisfy Watson. He turned to me.

"Get your PX squared away."

"It's not mine," I reminded him. The PX was actually under his jurisdiction. "I've tried to get stock by calling a colonel on your staff."

The general said again, "Get things squared away."

As we walked out of the PX, he stopped and looked around. It was a brutally hot day.

He said, "You don't have any shade in this battalion." I thought at first I had misunderstood him. I hadn't. He repeated his statement again, "Get some shade in here for the troops." He walked toward his sedan. I thought to myself, thank God. If he ever wants to see the NCO/EM club, I'll really be in trouble. The place was overflowing every day. We couldn't even cool the beer fast enough. The soldiers just drank it warm.

As he was getting into his sedan, he turned and said, "I'll be back." I thought, don't be in a hurry, you silly shit.

I went into my office and tried the PX chain of command once again. Finally I got a colonel on the phone. I told him of the general's wish. "I can give you a few ribbons," he said, "but that's all I have in the system. I'll send someone down with them."

But the big challenge was what to do about the shade.

Fred came in to ask me something and I put the question to him. He didn't have a solution. On his way out, he said, "Too bad we're not paratroopers. Then we'd have some chutes."

"That's it!" I said, "You're a genius!" He looked surprised. Charlie Connell had been telling me for months about a cargo parachute he had appropriated from someone. He wanted it for his family room at home, and he had told me about it so many times, I had begun to tune him out. I called Charlie.

"I need your parachute. It's a matter of my career." I told him what had happened.

"I'll bring it right down." Soon, he arrived with the chute in the back of his jeep. "How are you going to hang it?"

"Right on the flag pole in front of the PX."

We had it up in a few hours, and it was perfect. To my surprise, even the transients—not usually the souls of cooperation—helped move the picnic tables under it. Later, a trooper arrived from the PX in Long Binh with fifty commendation ribbons—enough to last about ten minutes. I gave them to the PX manager with instructions not to put them out for sale until he saw General Watson come through the door. Then I called in the sergeant major.

"Get four helmet liners. Go out and choose four returning NCOs. Give them the liners to wear and an area they are responsible for policing. If they're manifested to leave, then they must pass the duty and liner on to other NCOs."

Two days later, General Watson returned. The policing was better but not up to his standards. He was surprised and pleased with the parachute. The charade with the ribbons worked. He departed, muttering words of praise.

On the morning of April 30th I awoke with a funny feeling. It was 0600, and I had been in bed only a few hours. We had taken the last convoy out to the airport at 0200. It meant that everyone was truly gone, and I had to get up to see if it was really true.

I walked through the Headquarters building. There was no one there, and the phones were silent. I went out to the street. Not one living soul in sight. It took me aback. I had never seen the area empty. Becoming concerned about the security at the front gate, I got into a jeep and drove up there. There were two guards at the gate, both dressed in civilian clothes. The engineering outfit had indeed taken over for us, and the MPs had been booked out on the last plane. It felt strange to have outsiders protecting the area.

Within the Officers' Company or Headquarters Company, I found no one. I went back to the Headquarters building. Still no one. I noticed smoke coming from the 259th's mess hall chimney. I walked over to get a cup of coffee. All strangers. The cooks belonged to the new tenant. I walked up the main street and passed the PX, where the parachute was flapping in the breeze. I went up to the end and back around past the barbershop and steam bath. Still, not a soul. I returned to the mess hall, got another cup of coffee, went across the street, and sat down on a fifty-five-gallon drum. I had to smile. This had been a favorite spot for returnees to idle away their final hours.

The silence was overwhelming. Eventually, the sergeant major joined me on the drum next to me.

"How do you think we did?" I asked.

He said, "We did damn good. They're all gone, aren't they?"

"I'd better call the AG and the DCSPER and tell them."

"I'll get the troops moving," he replied.

"Assemble everyone outside the Headquarters building in about an hour," I told him.

It took three different telephone numbers to raise someone in the DCSPER's office. I reported that everyone had departed—there were no transients left in the battalion. A call to the AG with the same report was greeted with a gratifying, "Nice job."

The troopers that assembled outside Headquarters were armed with brooms. There were only about sixty people left. I congratulated them on their performance. They said they were ready to clean out the buildings—they wanted to get on with it so they could catch an evening plane out of Alpha to the States. Everyone could go home with the exception of the supply personnel, who would have to hang around to inventory the place and turn the equipment over to the new tenants.

The men were dead-tired, but like the thousands of people they had processed, they could smell home. They worked fast and efficiently. By mid-afternoon, the buildings were swept clean and the grounds policed up. I told the sergeant major to saddle them up and get them over to Alpha. We loaded our last bus with what was left of the 90th. Fred said goodbye and we promised to get together back in the States.

When the bus went through the front gate, there were nine of us left: Lieutenant Worth, his staff, and the three company supply sergeants. Two of the special services women remained, faced with the similar task of turning in their equipment. Our final job was ahead of us—hand the place off to the engineers.

CHAPTER 9
GOING HOME

Lieutenant Worth and his people began the joint inventory with supply personnel from the civilian engineering group. Now that the pressure was off to out-process soldiers, I suddenly realized how difficult the inventory might be. This outfit had been here for six years, and in that time it had had twelve previous commanders and countless supply people. Undoubtedly, the books contained errors. All of it was going to take longer than I had thought.

The initial step was to count all the buildings and compare the count against the list provided by the USARV post engineer. I came up one short because of the building that had collapsed in the motor pool area. But I also had three buildings not on the list. Of course, one was the pee house. No one had ever updated the records, so we called it even.

While Lieutenant Worth and company were inventorying equipment, I put the finishing touches on the unit's history and on the battalion's meritorious unit citation. Then I could no longer put it off. I turned back to the inventory task. Taking stock of a unit this size was not an easy task. We had almost fifteen thousand bedsheets and a similar number of kitchen utensils. The most difficult items to inventory were communications gear. We had all the Army's various radios and field telephones, and they were scattered all over the battalion.

We turned in all our weapons and ammunition. We were lucky with the ammo, since the Vietnamese had taken over the operation of the ammo dump and had accepted everything, including all our loose rounds. If the Americans had still been running the show, they would have accepted only unopened cases. The policy was the same everywhere. The unit turning in ammo would have to take care of the loose rounds on its own. I never could understand the reasoning, because it led to unsafe storage. As a result, most stateside units have a cache of ammo buried somewhere out in the training area.

The PX manager was moving his stock back to the main PX on Long Binh, while the club NCOs were doing the same with their liquor supplies. The special services woman had to move three pool tables to the service club at the USARV headquarters. No one was left to drive the truck, so I ended up doing it myself.

As I walked past the Tactical Operations Center (TOC), I noticed that some sandbags had fallen away from one of the containers we used as the wall of the TOC—containers used for shipping cargo. I noticed that the fallen sandbags had exposed a container's door. I opened it and looked. Inside were key punch machines, computer paper, and IBM punch cards. By the look of things, it had all been stored there for years. I knew none of it was on my books, so I closed the door and restacked the sandbags myself. If that stuff had been counted during the inventory, I would have been faced with a mountain of paperwork.

Each day I would check with Lieutenant Worth to see how the inventory was going. We tried to be positive about the growing list of shortages by saying that no big item—like a truck—had come up. But I had been around the Army long enough to know that no matter what the size or value of an item, the paperwork was about the same—nightmarish. I began to think of what the battalion had on hand that we could use as trade bait.

Soon the PX and clubs were empty and closed. All the other buildings that the new unit would not use were locked up. As the population of the civilians grew, we began to feel out of place. Each visit to the mess hall brought its share of stares and asides, "When is the Army getting out of here?"

The fighting at An Loc had ended. ARVN, with a lot of material help from the Americans, had turned back the North Vietnamese. Nevertheless, I still felt uncomfortable not having control over the compound's security.

Lieutenant Worth came into my office on the sixth day to announce that the inventory was complete. The civilians wanted to meet with me to discuss the shortages and sign the property over to them. I looked over the list. It was long, but there were also a lot of overages. We were missing six EE8 telephones and two PRC6 radios, but we had an extra PRC-10 radio. The item that really jumped off the page was a fifty-gallon coffeemaker. How the hell could we be short a coffeemaker that was part of the steam table?

Worth said, "It's a paper mix-up. We probably had turned it in when we closed down the mess hall in the 18th Replacement Company."

I said, "What do you mean, probably? Did we or didn't we?" He said he wasn't the S-4 when the mess had been turned in. I thought, how many times have I heard that excuse here in 'Nam? Another favorite was, "Don't ask me, I'm new here." Like magic, this excuse would turn to, "Don't ask me, I'm short," after the six-month mark in a soldier's tour.

So I asked Worth, "Will the engineers bargain overages against shortages?"

"Yeah," he said, "but we don't have enough overages to offset the items short."

"Set up a meeting," I said, and I walked across to the 259th arms room to check with Sergeant Adams. As I was returning to the battalion headquarters, Charlie drove up to get his parachute. I had it taken down and refolded for him.

After we put it in the jeep, he said, "I'm getting a drop, and I'll be going home in a couple of days. I'd like to go home via Hawaii and spend some time with you. Could you arrange for my flight to Hawaii on the leave plane, rather than to Travis in California?"

"Sure," I said.

He asked, "When are you going to Hawaii?" I told him of the shortage problem. "If things don't go well this afternoon, I might be here all summer."

That afternoon in my office, the engineers sat on one side of the table. Worth, his sergeant, and I sat on the other. This table had been a silent witness to some of the most important conversations in my life.

The engineers' opening remarks set the tone. Apparently, we 'Army guys' were not going to put anything over on them. I was not much predisposed to like them, either. This same contracting group had done a lot of the construction in Vietnam, but whenever I had called upon them to make a repair to the compound, they always had an excuse for not doing the work. It gave me pleasure to think they were going to live in the area they had neglected for so many years.

We were able to do some horse-trading, but the list of overages was soon depleted. They wanted me to sign things over immediately, with all the shortages annotated. Then the discrepancies would become my problem and not theirs. Before I would sign anything, however, I asked their supply chief to step outside with me. He looked puzzled, but he got up and followed me.

I went straight across the street to the 259th supply room with him in tow. Inside was Sergeant Adams.

"Open up the arms room," I said. The civilians had never gone inside before. We had already turned our weapons in directly to the depot. Sergeant Adams undid the locks and stepped in to turn on the light. I asked my civilian guest to go in. He did, and when he looked around, he beamed. There on one wall were approximately fifty Colt .45 army pistols, and on the other wall were their holsters.

"Will these help?" I asked.

"Are they yours?" he asked.

"Possession is nine-tenths of the law," I replied. "They're mine, and they're not on the books, so no one else knows about them."

He asked the unforgivable question: "Where did you get them?"

I didn't answer but turned and began to walk out of the room. He followed me all the way back to my office.

When we were both seated again, he began to fill in the inventory sheet, checking all the right spaces. The others just stared at him. When he finished, the 90th had been turned over to the engineers—with everything in order.

Using these forms, Worth was able to close each company's supply books. I took them to Headquarters, made Xerox copies for my personal files, and turned them into the post supply officer. With the necessary receipts, I rode back to the 90th, singing as loud as I could. In the five-mile journey, I did not see another vehicle. I passed many deserted buildings, motor pools, maintenance shops, and warehouses. Not a soul in sight. I felt as if I were the last American left in Vietnam.

I called the AG, Colonel Wagner. "I've just completed the turn in for the unit."

"Well, go home at any time," he said.

"I'll leave the day after tomorrow, so you can make the change of command order between Major Charles and myself effective May 8th."

That night, Colonel Wagner invited me to have dinner at the USARV general officers' mess. He said Charlie had also been invited to come. Worth and his supply people were getting ready to leave for Alpha the next morning.

That evening I met Charlie in the mess lobby. Colonel Wagner waved us into the bar and bought us a drink. As the room filled with new arrivals, everyone stopped by to wish us well. At 1900 hours, like magic, we headed into the dining room.

Who was there but General McDowell. He asked us to sit at his table. After all my trials with him, his was the last table I'd pick— but the decision wasn't mine. To his credit, he was a gracious host, and I even found myself laughing as he retold the helicopter story. At the end of the meal, he rose from his seat to say a few words. For the audience, he reviewed our accomplishments: first Charlie's and then mine. He had nothing but accolades for us. When he finished, the people gave us a standing round of applause. After dinner, he bought us drinks at the bar. There, he said his goodbyes, wished us well, and left.

I was beginning to feel self-conscious in the middle of all the rank. A glance at Charlie showed he was feeling the same way. After a respectable amount of time, I whispered, "Let's get the hell out of here."

He nodded and we sought out Colonel Wagner, paid our respects, and took our leave. We decided to head back to the

90th. I had a feeling Worth and his people would be in the middle of a farewell party.

The drive back was eerie. This usually active place was quiet as a church. But sure enough, Worth and the four sergeants, plus the two special services women, were having a party in the trailer area. Everyone had brought out whatever liquor they had left, and one of the picnic tables was now a bar. They had eaten a kingly meal: steak, chicken, and even shrimp—better fare than Charlie and I had eaten. The party went on and on. Everybody had war stories to tell. Charlie and I killed a bottle of scotch. Sometime in the early morning hours, I took all the palm trees out of their pots and filled up Charlie's sedan with them, with the exception of the driver's seat.

When the scotch ran out, Charlie decided to leave. He was in no shape to drive, but I couldn't persuade him to stay over. He got in his sedan without noticing the plants. He pulled away, his head surrounded by swaying palms.

I awoke the next morning wishing I were dead. I had to get up and go to USARV. Both Charlie and I were to receive the Legion of Merit medal that morning. I felt I was doing everything in slow motion—time was going by, but no matter what I told myself, I couldn't get moving. In fact, every once in a while, I would have to sit down to rest. I told myself that once I got outside, I would feel better. But as I got in the jeep, I knew I'd been kidding myself.

I got to Colonel Wagner's office about ten minutes before the appointed time. There was no sign of Charlie. Colonel Wagner asked if I had seen him that morning, and I lied and said no. Just about then, Charlie walked in. I took a glance and hoped I didn't look that bad.

The ceremony was to be held down the hall in one of the big offices. As we followed the colonel, Charlie fell in and whispered to me, "You son of a bitch. Those fucking trees you put in the sedan destroyed my clean uniform this morning." It seems he hadn't noticed them this morning and had jumped into the muddy driver's seat.

The ceremony was endless. On one occasion, I thought it was lights out for me, but I was able to lean slightly against a wall and still look as if I were at attention. After the ceremony, someone wheeled in a big cake and coffee. The sight of the cake almost put me over the top, but a sip of the coffee helped.

After we got outside in the parking lot, Charlie was still grousing.

"Take your medal off," I said. "You look like you're showboating." He grinned and put it back in the box. He wouldn't admit it, but his hangover was as bad as mine. He departed saying he would see me that night at Alpha. Tomorrow we would both be on our way for Hawaii.

I returned to the 90th to pick up my possessions and the battalion colors. Lieutenant Worth and his people had already left. The women from special services were pulling away just as I got to the trailer. A final goodbye, and they were gone. I was the only one left. After loading the jeep, I took a last walk around. The battalion was beginning to fill up with civilians.

My next stop was a final check around the Headquarters building. I picked up the colors and returned to the jeep. As I drove out of the front gate, I stopped for one final look. All of a sudden the year I spent here seemed like the shortest and longest of my life all at the same time. Could all that have occurred in just one year?

It would be a long time digesting, and I said aloud, "I better get the hell out of here fast."

Since I had forgotten to bring the text for the unit's award earlier in the day, I had to stop by USARV Headquarters. I walked in the office marked "Awards and Decorations." It was a huge place, but to my surprise, no one was in sight. A few months ago, hundreds of people would have been here. I yelled out, and a voice from the far end said, "Back here." At the back of the office, I came upon a soldier sitting at a desk that was totally covered with paper stacked three feet high.

"I want to turn in a recommendation for a unit award."

"Put it on top of the pile on the left-hand side."

"Are you the only one left in the office?" I asked.

"No, the sergeant has gone for some chow." There was nothing to do but place the paper on top of the pile.

Leaving Headquarters, I hoped that the traffic on Route 1 would be light. But upon pulling out into the traffic, I realized my wish would not come true. My last ride down Route 1 was, like the others, a blur. As I pulled up to the front gate of Alpha, the MP signaled me to stop. He saluted.

"Who are you?"

Shocked, I said, "Your battalion commander."

He flushed. "Sorry. I've just been assigned to the 178th." I drove on to the compound and parked the jeep. Taking the colors, I walked up the steps to the orderly room. The office seemed busier than usual, but I recognized no one.

Major Charles came out of his office and noticed me standing there. I hoped my expression didn't give away the fact that I was feeling like a lost soul. He took the colors and led me into his office.

I asked him how things were going. Since I was still the battalion commander, I felt it was my duty to know what was going on. As we talked about one thing and another, I felt my mind wandering. I was dreaming of Hawaii, so I was really not absorbing what he was telling me. Only ten days ago, I had my finger on everything going on here or at Long Binh. Charles seemed to sense my short attention span, and he excused himself.

After he left, I thought that perhaps I was still feeling the effects of last night's party. I went out to walk around the compound. The faces in the mess hall were new. The processing NCOs were all unfamiliar, and they seemed to ignore me. I realized they were manifesting a flight. The few people who knew me would stop and talk, not about the processing, but about how lucky I was to be going home. Finally, Major Charles found me in the processing building and asked if I had given my urine sample. I hadn't. He suggested I do so if I wanted to depart the next day. I pretended I had that on my list of things to do. After he left, the irony struck me. How could I, of all people, forget about the sample?

I waited my turn at the urinalysis point. As I stepped up to give my sample, a voice yelled out, "Step up closer, #4."

I stepped up closer.

After giving my sample, I walked over to the air-conditioned BOQ. It felt good to get inside. I sat down, cracked a can of Coke, and began to wonder what was wrong with me. I didn't seem go give a shit about anything but getting out. As I sat there, I began to realize that I was no longer a member of the family. I was now a transient.

I must have fallen asleep. The next thing I knew, Connie and Jack were calling to me to have a beer with them at the small BOQ bar. One beer led to another, and one war story after another.

Connie said he had a story to tell me. He had been waiting for months for the right time. The day I had left for Hawaii for R&R, General Martin had dropped by to wish everyone a Merry Christmas. There was no one in the Headquarters building but Fred and Connie. The general had walked right into Fred's office, where they were sitting, and he stayed about five or ten minutes, just passing the time. After Martin left, Connie had gotten up and started to pace back and forth. My office was dark, but because the door between the two offices was open, as Connie paced, he walked right in and then back out. He said his heart almost stopped when he realized what he had just seen—there, on my couch, which was flush with the wall that separated Fred's office from mine, were my driver and his Vietnamese girlfriend naked as the day they were born. Connie said he started to chew the trooper out, but for some reason, he couldn't stop laughing—or was it crying? Every time he thought of Martin just inches away from this scene, he began laughing more hysterically. The driver and the girl got dressed and beat a hasty exit. He said neither Fred nor he ever had the courage to tell me—not to protect the driver, but to protect me. They felt I had enough to worry about.

The three of us went out to dinner at the Vietnamese officers' club at Tan Son Nhut. During dinner, I reminded them that we were breaking the rules again—all of us were off the compound at the same time. But I really didn't care, and the meal was good.

When we got back, the duty officer told me, "Charlie called to say he would be delayed a day. Will you wait for him?" I called him and said I would, but later that night, I changed my mind and said, "Fuck it, I'm leaving tomorrow!" I justified my betrayal by deciding that I would pick him up at the airport in Hawaii.

At midnight, I conducted the change-of-command ceremony with Major Charles. It was not as glamorous as mine a year ago, but the effect was the same—a changing of the guard. At the stroke of midnight, I removed my green tabs and placed them on Charles. Then I turned to Connie, who handed me the colors. I handed them to Charles. Everyone applauded and had a comment, most of which were delivered with slurred speech.

Charles and I had been stiffly formal but now we both broke into laughter.

"I said, 'It's all yours.'" I really wanted to shout, "I made it. I did it!" But I was a bit self-conscious. The party started to warm up, and the first to drop out was Major Charles, saying he had things to check on. I thought to myself, that was me just a while ago.

The next morning I again rose in pain, but nothing like the morning before. Hours passed slowly. I couldn't wait to get on that plane, and each second that passed until then brought on a rush of wild thoughts. "What if the place gets mortared? I don't want to die on my last day. Where would I go to protect myself? I should stay out of crowds." Then another voice assured me, "Nothing can happen now." I began to understand why some people—especially the ones who tested positive—reacted so violently when told they were going to the detox center, or even when they heard that their flight was delayed.

It was finally time to dress. After almost a year of fatigues and boots, khakis and low quarters felt strange. And without the green tabs, my uniform felt naked.

Connie and Jack were having breakfast as I arrived in the mess. Connie suggested that I go out in style and use the VIP lounge. The lounge was only to be used by full colonels and above. And at Alpha, it actually looked and felt like a VIP lounge.

"There is only one colonel booked on the flight to Hawaii," Connie coaxed.

So I said, "Why not?"

We walked across the compound and into the processing building. A few old-timers were there to say goodbye. After hearing the last farewells, we headed toward the VIP lounge. As we walked through the door, my heart stopped. Seated in the lounge was Colonel Mack. Too late to retreat. He had looked up from his book and spotted me. "Hello, Bill," he said.

Oh shit, I thought. I had worked for him for about a year in Hawaii, and during that time, we hadn't agreed on a single thing, including the presence of a peace symbol on a re-enlistment poster—in fact, the very poster that was now hanging right over his head.

Our conversation was strained. Soon we both gave up and began to read. Connie poked his head in and said it was time to go. He said my driver would take me to the plane.

Colonel Mack said, "No sense taking two vehicles. I'll ride along with you, Bill." Connie and I exchanged a look. How the hell would I shake him to get into the first class section?

We got into the sedan, and I made a few remarks to my driver about how comfortable my office couch had been. To my delight, his neck reddened just as Colonel Mack's face registered bafflement. The driver wished me well and said he would look me up after he came stateside. He did.

As the car stopped next to the 747, both Mack and I got out. My mind was racing, trying to come up with a way to get into first class without Colonel Mack. Mack had exited the passenger's side and began to walk toward the staircase at the back of the plane. I stayed on the other side and started chewing out the driver.

"Look at the condition of this vehicle, dirty inside and out. Look at yourself." All the while I was looking sideways, watching Mack. He seemed to be taking forever. He was a big man and moved slowly. I went on, "Look at those boots. When was the last time a cloth hit those, Mister? Your brass." The expression on the driver's face was one of amazement. I had never criticized him like this before, and in reality, he and the car both looked pretty good. But of course Mack loved to see people being chewed out—he was a perfectionist. No one could please him.

Just about the time I had run out of things to criticize, Mack disappeared into the plane. The minute he did, I said to the driver, "Forget everything after hello." I shook his hand, and he began to realize why I had gone through my act. We both grinned.

I said, "We are all actors, some bad, others good. That colonel is a bad actor." I took off up the steps to the front cabin—two steps at a time.

As I reached the door, the stewardess said, "You're really in a hurry." "Yes, I am!" In a few moments, after I was safely buckled in, the doors were closed and the plane began to taxi out on the runway. Because they made good targets, these flights got immediate clearance to leave. In another few minutes, we were off. There was a loud cheer from the back.

I settled back in my seat feeling tired, sad, and elated all at once.

I said aloud, "It's done!"

CPSIA information can be obtained
at www.ICGtesting.com
Printed in the USA
LVHW02s0221160518
577376LV00026B/1159/P